America at Risk

America at Risk

The Crisis of Hope, Trust, and Caring

Robert Perrucci and Carolyn C. Perrucci

ROWMAN & LITTLEFIELD PUBLISHERS, INC.
Lanham • Boulder • New York • Toronto • Plymouth, UK

ROWMAN & LITTLEFIELD PUBLISHERS, INC.

Published in the United States of America
by Rowman & Littlefield Publishers, Inc.
A wholly owned subsidary of The Rowman & Littlefield Publishing Group, Inc.
4501 Forbes Boulevard, Suite 200, Lanham, Maryland 20706
www.rowmanlittlefield.com

Estover Road
Plymouth PL6 7PY
United Kingdom

British Library Cataloguing in Publication Information Available

Library of Congress Cataloging-in-Publication Data:

Perrucci, Robert.
America at risk: the crisis of hope, trust, and caring / Perrucci, Robert, and
Carolyn C. Perrucci.
     p. cm.
   Includes bibliographical references and index.
   ISBN 978-0-7425-6369-8 (cloth : alk. paper) — ISBN 978-0-7425-6370-4 (pbk. :
alk. paper) — ISBN 978-0-7425-6632-3 (electronic)
   1. United States—Social conditions—1980– 2. United States--Economic
conditions—2001– 3. Social classes—United States. I. Perrucci, Carolyn
Cummings. II. Title.
   HN59.2.P464 2009
   306.0973'09051—dc22   2009000526

Printed in the United States of America

♾ ™ The paper used in this publication meets the minimum requirements of
American National Standard for Information Sciences—Permanence of Paper for
Printed Library Materials, ANSI/NISO Z39.48-1992.

For American workers

Contents

Preface: Why We Wrote This Book

This book is the latest effort in a thirty-year project to understand the most significant transformation of American society since the Industrial Revolution. This transformation was first identified in an extended and systematic way by Barry Bluestone and Bennett Harrison, in their *The Deindustrialization of America*, 1982, and has continued to develop with many unforeseen consequences for all segments of American society. Our initial effort to examine this transformation was in a study of plant closings in the mid- to late 1970s, in Carolyn C. Perrucci, Robert Perrucci, Dena B. Targ, and Harry R. Targ, *Plant Closings: International Context and Social Costs*, 1988, 2005.

The loss of jobs in the automobile industry and the movement of production abroad were accompanied by increased foreign investment in the United States, initially by the Japanese automobile industry. This development was identified in Robert Perrucci, *Japanese Auto Transplants in the Heartland: Corporatism and Community*, 1994.

As more and more high-wage, blue-collar jobs were lost to offshoring and technological change, it became apparent that the U.S. class structure was also changing, most significantly by the decline of the middle class. This significant development was the subject of Robert Perrucci and Earl Wysong, *The New Class Society: Goodbye, American Dream?*, 1999, 2003, 2008, which serves as the foundation for our current book on the crisis in America. *The New Class Society* described the emergence of a polarized society with a prosperous privileged class, a shrinking middle class, and an insecure working class, with historically unprecedented disparities in income and wealth and declining opportunities for improvement in job security, wages, and a better life for the next generation. The cumulative impact of this polarized society on the average American over the last thirty years or so has been the loss of hope for a better future, the decline in trust for our mainstream institutions, and the declining support for government programs that express help and caring for those who live on the fringes of society.

The far-reaching effects of economic change, technological change, and organizational change extended to all levels and sectors of the workplace, family life, and community life. We attempted to capture these developments in Carolyn C. Perrucci and Dena B. Targ, *Marriage and the Family: A Critical Analysis and Proposals for Change*, 1973, and Robert Perrucci and Carolyn C. Perrucci, *The Transformation of Work in the New Economy*, 2007.

Our concern in this book is to identify how the broad economic and technological forces have changed the way Americans think about themselves, their future, and the lives of their children and neighbors. Although not yet well understood, we believe what has occurred has been a change in belief in oneself and a belief in social institutions that we have chosen to refer to as a decline in hope, trust, and caring. We believe that hope, trust, and caring are essential for healthy individuals and that a healthy society creates conditions for their realization. Our central thesis is that hope, trust, and caring are interconnected. The erosion of one leads to the erosion of others, and an improvement in one can lead to improvement in others. Thus, the solutions that we propose are designed to build hope (jobs and wages) that can lead to greater trust of institutions and leaders and can expand the spirit of caring for the less fortunate by reducing opposition to government programs to help marginalized Americans. Our solutions also try to encourage partnerships between citizens and government that can create positive cycles of hope, trust, and caring.

This book was conceptualized in 2007, and as we worked on the book throughout 2008, we often felt that the various candidates in the primaries and election were peeking into our manuscript and using our ideas. The election is now behind us, and this book is not specifically about the 2008 presidential campaign or Wall Street crisis, although both are relevant to our argument. Rather, we draw on data and trends over the last thirty years in America to focus on the loss of hope, trust, and caring more broadly, and offer recommendations for change.

OUR APPROACH

The authors' approach in this book is *critical sociology*, which has two distinctive features: (1) a focus on the dominant economic, political, and cultural institutions as the source of the main social problems afflicting Americans; and (2) a belief that knowledge of the social world enhances consciousness and stimulates human action to change society in ways that further human fulfillment. Thus, we hope that our analysis of events over the last thirty years will enlighten working Americans to see the institutional conditions that have produced their present human condition and will motivate them to act on behalf of their individual and collective interests.

The conditions that we identify as the source of social problems are also the product of the values that we endorse. Although empirical research evidence about social conditions is important for identifying social problems, ultimately we rely on our value preferences to guide the selection of what we present to the reader in this book. Our own values and preferences are based on assumptions about what makes for a healthy human being and a healthy society. In our view, healthy individuals must have resources to meet their basic physical needs, and they must feel free of future insecurity regarding those resources. Healthy individuals must be fully informed about the policy decisions that affect their daily lives and they should have the opportunity to express their views about policy in public meetings with elected officials or in computerized referenda. Finally, a healthy society encourages the development of individuals who will contribute to the well being of other members of society.

Our approach also includes policy proposals that we believe can contribute to a healthy individual and a healthy society. The choice of these particular policies is also based on value preferences and a belief that these policies can help to shape social institutions that will better serve the American people. Our view of the value preferences that can guide new social policies was expressed in a January 11, 1944, message to Congress on the State of the Union when President Franklin Delano Roosevelt called for a second Bill of Rights that proposed a new basis for security and prosperity:

> The right to a useful and remunerative job in the industries or shops or farms or mines of the nation;
> The right to earn enough to provide adequate food and clothing and recreation;
> The right of every family to a decent home;
> The right to adequate medical care and the opportunity to achieve and enjoy good health;
> The right to adequate protection from the economic fears of old age, sickness, accident, and unemployment;
> The right to a good education.

We thank anonymous reviewers for their comments and criticisms, and especially Jack Niemonen for extensive and helpful comments on an earlier draft. We thank our coauthors of other books, Earl Wysong, Dena Targ, Harry Targ, and Lee Trachtman, for their indirect contributions to this work. Carolyn Perrucci thanks Purdue University for a sabbatical leave for the spring semester 2008. We also thank our editor, Alan McClare, for his support of the project and contributions to its development, our associate editor Sarah Stanton for helping us shape the final draft and guiding the project to completion, and Lynn Weber for her contributions as production editor.

1

Diagnosis: How the New Economy Has Eroded Hope, Trust, and Caring

There is a strong feeling across the land that something is amiss in America. You sometimes hear about these feelings when people discuss their concerns about how the baby boom generation is going to bankrupt our social security or Medicare programs, or about the growing size of the national debt that will be paid for by future generations. Concerns about these programs are real and important, but they are often part of a deeper sense of insecurity that Americans have about their future that are difficult to put into words. In conversations with friends and casual acquaintances we frequently hear them saying: *Something is wrong with America,* or *This isn't the America I grew up in. I don't recognize it anymore.* Even solicitations for money or requests for signatures on petitions from political organizations begin with an angry phrase like: *Let's take this country back! Our country is run by criminals and liars, the opposition party lacks a backbone, and the corporate-controlled media gave up on reporting most real news a long time ago.*[1] Some may respond to these charges by saying: *So what's new, Americans have always grumbled about what's wrong with their country.* That's probably true, but the statement refers to experiences within the speaker's lifetime. People have been grumbling about conditions in America, and they have been doing so with increasing shrillness, *especially in the last thirty years.* Something is amiss in America. What is it? Can we begin to identify some of the symptoms of the collective *angst* that seems to plague America? We want to try to answer some of these questions, so let's begin.

Initially, let's dismiss any crazy notions about why America is in trouble. We don't believe that America's problems are due to any purposely developed plan by some malevolent group to bring down America. People do conspire to harm those they dislike or to advance their interests, but

1

they tend to do so on a much smaller scale. We think it is more useful to search for the problems facing our country in its recent history, and in its economic, political, and social institutions. The American people and their collective institutions comprise an enormously complex society, or what a French sociologist once called *Le grand etre*, The Great Being. And although a society is not a living organism, it does, like all living things, evolve and change in response to conditions in its environment. Observing the evolutionary process for a human society is not a pretty sight, because not everything changes in a smooth, consistent fashion. There are many things that often seem out of sync—ideas or practices that are better suited to an earlier time in a country's history and just don't work well today. A sociologist named William Ogburn referred to this condition as *cultural lag*, or the difficulty that people have in modifying their behavior to fit the new conditions or the challenges facing governmental or social organizations when trying to modify their practices to face new conditions. During the twentieth century, American society experienced a broad range of changes that have transformed social institutions and the way that people live. To name some of the more obvious change agents: electricity, telephone, internal combustion engine, assembly line, television, air travel, nuclear energy, heart transplants, cloning, computers, Internet, and on and on—all in the last hundred years. These innovations have transformed the way people work, who works, their family life, and they have generated new laws, regulations, and social practices to adapt to the new innovations. But the social adaptations have been messy, and they will continue to be messy. It is this *messiness* that creates a condition of *social strain* in human affairs that is the basis for what ails America. Wide-ranging scientific and technical innovations have transformed how people live *within their lifetime*, making it especially difficult for people to adapt and for social institutions to change rapidly enough to deal with time-based dislocations. In the past, change was much slower, often occurring across generations, and thereby making adaptation easier.

There are probably many conditions that can erode hope, trust, and caring in a society. For example, an acute crisis like the 9/11 attack, or the 2008 Wall Street crisis can make people fearful and insecure about the future. Another example would be how the traditional American value of individualism can reduce a sense of caring and responsibility to help others. However, our emphasis is elsewhere, namely, long-standing chronic conditions that have gradually affected the social body and the American spirit. We believe that the cumulative consequence of rapid social change that has occurred over the last thirty years has exposed Americans and their institutions to greater strain and has produced three outcomes that are so potentially harmful that they have led us to claim that America is at a critical juncture in its history. The three outcomes or products of rapid social change are *latent,* in that they lie below the level of immediate consciousness, but they are ever-present in shaping social life. To use a medical metaphor, the three conditions act like low-grade chronic infections, and if left untreated, will produce continued decline in the health and well being of persons and social institutions. We refer to these three conditions as *deficiencies in hope, trust, and caring.* We believe that hope, trust, and caring are necessary for a healthy human being and that they are the vital signs of health. And we further believe that a healthy society is one in which its institutions facilitate the experience of hope, trust, and caring in its members.

We believe that the decline of hope, trust, and caring is the unanticipated consequence of the major transformation over the last thirty years in the kind of goods and services produced in America, in the technology that is used in production, and in the people who are involved in the production process. We call the composite of these changes the *new economy.* The new economy made its appearance in the mid-1970s, beginning with the slow but steady decline in the manufacturing sector of the economy. Although production plants in the auto, steel, and textile industries were being closed, no one seemed to notice because there was an expansion of jobs in the service sector and a growing demand for people to fill professional, technical, and managerial occupations. It took a while for people to realize that most of the jobs that were being created were low-wage service jobs in food preparation and service, janitorial services, hospital and nursing home services, and retail sales. Workers in relatively high-wage, often unionized, jobs, with pensions and health insurance, were being replaced by jobs with little security and no benefits.

A second feature of the *new economy* is the expanded role of computer-based technology in many different sectors of the economy, such as manufacturing, banking and financial services, customer services, and mid-level, white-collar, paper-processing jobs. The new computer-based technology had the benefit of increased productivity, which meant that more work could be done with fewer workers. Aiding the use of computer-based technology were new innovations in telecommunications that made it possible to communicate, coordinate, and control activities and people who were working in geographically separated places. This provided the means for the geographical dispersion of the production and delivery of goods and services. American companies could now produce a car, a refrigerator, a computer, or clothing in factories scattered around the globe using workers from many different countries.

The third feature of the *new economy* is the use of new ways of organizing work and controlling workers. This change is reflected in the increased use of self-directed work teams, whose members are cross-trained to carry out each other's tasks and are guided by continuous improvement goals requiring team members to work smarter and faster. It also involves the use of nonstandard work arrangements based on part-time and temporary workers. An additional aspect of the new work organization is the use of computer-guided control of work flow and the continuous measurement of individual productivity. For example, in a plastic film plant that we recently studied, management used the practice of making daily postings on bulletin boards of how much product had been produced by each machine and each worker.[2] Similar techniques have been introduced into many data-entry jobs involving computers, whereby operators are *informed* by their machines if their keystroke rate is falling behind a set standard.[3] This level of detailed monitoring is made possible by the use of computer-based measurement of work flow. The combined effect of these innovations in work organization resulted in reduced job security and increased control of both blue-collar and white-collar workers.

We describe these key features of the *new economy* as involving (1) globalization of production and distribution of goods and services, (2) computer-based production technology and telecommunications, and (3) flexible organization of work and workers. Let us examine further how each of these new developments has changed American society.

GLOBALIZED PRODUCTION

Beginning in the mid-1970s, many countries whose industrial base had been destroyed in World War II had recovered and were now competing with U.S. firms. With many new players in the global economy, the U.S. rate of economic growth slowed. Many firms responded to their declining domestic profits by increasing their direct and indirect investment in foreign countries, thereby creating multinational subsidiaries of the U.S. parent firm. One result of this shift in investment for multinational firms was the realization of a higher rate of profit from foreign investments than for domestic operations. This increased the attractiveness of foreign investment for many U.S. firms.

In the pursuit of higher profit margins, the shift of investment to countries with lower wages, less regulation of industry, and nonunion environments resulted in the loss of millions of high-wage, unionized jobs held by American workers. While manufacturing jobs were being lost, millions of new jobs were being created in the service sector, where workers were employed for fewer hours per week and at lower wages.[4] The deindustrialization of America had begun, and it would continue at an accelerated pace into the twenty-first century through a variety of practices involving plant closings, downsizing, and outsourcing work overseas.

COMPUTERIZED PRODUCTION

The globalization of production could not have taken place without new computer-based production and new telecommunications technology. Computer-assisted design and computer-assisted manufacturing (CAD-CAM) made it possible to produce products abroad with a new international worker. Workers across the globe no longer needed high levels of literacy or numeracy to work in manufacturing because of the "smart" machines. The physical work and experience-based skills of the traditional factory worker were no longer at a premium, and lower-skilled foreign workers in factories around the globe who were not unionized and had limited skill-based or market-based power to demand better pay and working conditions could now be employed as "machine tenders." The skilled worker with market-based power based on their scarce supply was now replaced by less experienced and skilled workers who are not in short supply and thereby less powerful in their relations with employers.

The dispersal of production across the globe required the means to coordinate and manage the activities of many people in different plants across the globe. If General Motors was going to produce a "global car" from components produced in Detroit, Mexico, and the Philippines, it needed the means to oversee and manage these dispersed operations. Advances in satellite-based telecommunications and computer information systems, combined with CAD-CAM production, made it possible to build the engines in Detroit, transmissions in Mexico, tires in the Philippines, and to ship the products to yet another country for assembly into a finished automobile that could be sold in worldwide markets.

At the same time that computer-based work was eliminating jobs in the United States, and deskilling the workforce, it also created demand for a new class of "knowledge workers." These college-educated engineers, computer analysts, and technicians became the higher-wage "symbol analysts" who were essential for developing and maintaining the new production and telecommunications technology. These new college-educated technical professionals contribute to the growing income and wealth inequality generated by the new economy.

FLEXIBLE WORK ORGANIZATION

The third feature of the new economy is a set of practices that give companies greater flexibility in the type of workers they hire and in their work arrangements.[5] In the old economy there existed a "social contract" between employer and employee that was the basis for job security; this "contract" was a tacit agreement of continued employment for productive workers. In the new economy this agreement has been replaced by the continued pressure on firms to be competitive in their prices, innovations, and services, resulting in the use of corporate restructuring and downsizing that has resulted in greater job insecurity for blue-collar and white-collar workers. This insecurity was linked to the greater use of part-time and temporary employees and increased efforts to increase work intensity through the use of work teams. Although work teams may be more productive, they also increase work intensity through the use of peer pressure and group discipline and technical forms of control of the work flow.[6]

The new economy was accompanied by a new political philosophy about the proper role of government in American life that has been referred to as "neoliberal globalization."[7] This involves a reduced role for government in regulating corporations and the economy and in assisting those Americans who have been harmed by rapid economic change. For example, workers who have lost jobs due to plant closures and global competition are eligible for federal grants to support retraining or additional education and extended unemployment benefits. The neoliberal view places greater reliance on the market to solve problems and is more sympathetic to the idea that individuals are responsible for their own success and failure in the marketplace. Moreover, the neoliberal view believes that the new economy provides greater opportunities and therefore the government should not be in the business of worrying about winners and losers. While winners and losers were being sorted out, the social safety net was being rolled up, resulting in less government support for social welfare programs and public services.

The replacement of government programs with individual responsibility and market forces was the centerpiece of the neoliberal project, and it contributed to the currently popular practice of "privatization," which shifts the provision of public services to private firms operating on a for-profit basis. Examples of privatization are found in the area of public education, where there is continuing interest in providing alternatives to public schools. Edison School, Inc., a private sector school, enrolls over 50,000 students in over 1,000 schools that are run on a for-profit basis. Other examples of privatization of services from public to private providers are found in the areas of state highways, social welfare services, child welfare systems, and prisons. The governors of Pennsylvania and Indiana recently leased the Pennsylvania Turnpike (514 miles) and the Indiana Toll Road (157 miles) to foreign firms for seventy-five years in return for $12.8 billion for Pennsylvania and $3.8 billion for Indiana. The foreign firms will be responsible for operating and maintaining the highway in return for the toll revenue. Privatization of public services, from schools to highways, will seriously damage the social safety net for poorer and more vulnerable Americans, and it will threaten the job security of millions of public employees.

Public services in areas such as education, transportation, fire and police services, and town planning are provided to all citizens regardless of income. In cases where such services cannot be publicly provided or financed, government regulates them to guarantee quality service and fair use. The erosion of public services and a shift to private free-market services has contributed to a decline in the American people's confidence in their political institutions. Because of the decline in federal support for public programs, many states and local governments are saddled with responsibilities that they cannot afford without raising taxes. Thus, the expanded use of the private sector to deliver public services will continue to cut into the availability and quality of services to Americans and their communities, and it will undermine the unions that represent public employees and protect their wages, health, and pension benefits.

THE NEW ECONOMY AND THE 2008 WALL STREET CRISIS

We view the 2008 financial crisis, including the subprime mortgage scandal and the financial turmoil on Wall Street that affected the value of homes, threatened business investment, and harmed the retirement savings of millions of Americans, as the latest example of the failure of the "new economy." The unfolding of the new economy over the last thirty years has sharply reduced the role of the manufacturing sector and sharply increased the role of the service sector, including financial services. The 1980s witnessed the growth of investment banks that became household names: Merrill Lynch, Lehman Brothers, Bear Stearns, Morgan Stanley, Goldman Sachs, Citibank, Bank of America. At least four of these banks failed during the crisis, but not before their CEOs and their upper-level management took away millions in salary and bonuses. The growing importance of the financial sector as the new producer of wealth led many political leaders to believe that as long as the national economy was growing it didn't make much difference if the growth was coming from producing cars and home appliances or creating new schemes for financial investments. What many leaders failed to realize was that a truly healthy and vibrant economy depends upon having average consumers (the "middle class") who have secure jobs and the expectation of growing wages. In short, the benefits of economic growth and expanded wealth must be broadly shared. Painfully, we have learned that the "smartest guys in the room" were wrong. How did this happen? Here is our view of how this train wreck occurred.

During the last thirty years in the United States we have seen the largest transfer of wealth from bottom income groups to the top 20 percent of Americans. Year after year the income gap has widened between top and bottom income groups. According to a 2005 study by the Economic Policy

Institute, the after-tax income share of the top 20 percent of U.S. house-holds had grown to 47.9 percent, which was almost as much as the share of the bottom 80 percent.[8] This historic transfer of wealth is seen most dra-matically in a comparison of top corporate earners, like CEOs at large firms, and average workers. In 1980 the average total CEO compensation was forty-two times what average workers earned. In 1990 this ratio increased to 107:1, and in 2005 it rose to 411:1. While CEO pay increased tenfold, average annual incomes of production workers decreased slightly, while minimum-wage workers experienced a 30 percent decrease.[9]

This transfer of wealth occurred under both Democratic and Republi-can presidential and congressional control and was greatly facilitated by government actions. In 1999, under the Clinton administration, Congress repealed the Glass-Steagall Act, opening the way for banks to own other financial institutions and to underwrite and trade mortgage-backed se-curities. It also permitted the creation of lightly regulated "hedge funds," which served as investment vehicles for the superrich (investors with at least $5 million of net worth). This Wall Street scheme extended the op-portunity for banks, financial houses, Freddie Mac, and Fannie Mae to buy mortgages with money borrowed at low government rates and repackage them for sale at higher interest rates. While congressional committees responsible for oversight were either distracted or looking the other way, the financial organizations were "cooking the books" to conceal how little actual cash was behind all this leveraged investment. By December 2008, Congress has provided a $700 billion package of loans and other support for troubled banks and mortgage holders. All the major players—President Bush, President-elect Obama, Senate and House majority leaders Reid and Pelosi—and the mainstream media seem to be supportive of this plan to transfer more money from the American taxpayer to bail out Wall Street.

Of course, the government had to do something to prevent a loss of confidence in American financial institutions and a widespread collapse of markets in the United States and around the world. But there were other possibilities that might have used fewer taxpayer dollars and imposed greater costs on the institutions that were responsible for the crisis. The government's plan does little to change the rules of the game that favor the wealthy and privileged at the expense of working Americans.

ORGANIZATION OF THE BOOK

Up to this point we have made the argument that the new economy has had a negative impact upon most Americans and that it has affected their sense of hope, their feelings of trust, and their expectation of caring in a time of need. Let us now be more specific about what we mean by hope, trust, and caring and indicate how we will continue with our argument throughout the remainder of the book.

First, **Hope** is a positive feeling or emotion that is based on an assessment of one's current life experiences in different venues such as family, work, or community, and the expectation that the future will improve these experiences. A person may have very negative feelings about a current situation at home or at work but may expect an improvement in the future, and thereby be hopeful. Similarly, the situation may be reversed, and one may have limited hope because of current problems and diminished expectations about what the future will bring. Feelings of hope or lack of hope may extend beyond one's personal situation to an assessment of what the future may bring for one's children, other family members, neighbors, or associates at work. A feeling of hope might have little to do with one's personal situation or the situation of others, but may be based on a generalized optimism about one's country. For example, a person may believe that America is the kind of country where "anybody can become somebody." Thus, a general feeling of hope or hopelessness may be a composite of one's personal and future situation, expectations about what the future may hold for others, and a general sense of optimism about the future.

In chapter 2 of this book we examine data from 1975 to 2007, describing patterns of job loss and job growth in the changing occupational structure in the United States. We focus on what has happened to wages in the past thirty years, and what jobs have been eliminated and added to the workforce. We also examine changes in job security and health and pension benefits during the same period. We believe that most working Americans are experiencing an erosion of hope because of over thirty years of growing job insecurity. In chapter 3, we also examine the decline in the American Dream, with special attention to the opportunities for upward mobility. Special attention is devoted to the American educational system as a pathway for mobility. The combination of job losses, wage stagnation, and declining opportunity for upward mobility has also contributed to the disappearance of the middle class in America and to a polarized society made up of a "privileged class" of winners in the new economy and a much larger percentage of losers in the new economy because of their insecure jobs and limited income and savings.

Second, **Trust** is about relationships with others and can be divided between personal trust and generalized trust (chapters 4 and 5). Personal trust is the belief that one's family members, co-workers, or friends are truthful, honest, and reliable. In short, they can be counted on to "do the right thing" in their relationships with you. This may mean that they will fulfill commitments and obligations based on blood ties or long-standing friendship. Generalized trust is about what you expect from people in general, or people in positions of authority who make decisions that affect your life.

Do you trust the younger generation to be honest, hardworking citizens or parents? Do you trust politicians to make policies that are in the best interest of average Americans? Do you trust the police, newspapers, corporate executives, and the Supreme Court? It is possible for a person to have high levels of personal trust but very little generalized trust. This may happen because of very strong familial or ethnic-religious ties, which produces high trust among in-group members but low trust of the out-group.

In chapter 4 we focus on national poll data concerning Americans' confidence in their institutions. We focus primarily on the loss of trust in government, political leadership, and corporations. We trace the source of this decline to the actions of government and corporations that led to massive job losses linked to free-trade policies. In chapter 5 we argue that the decline in confidence in major American institutions has led to a search for security in ethnic and religious groups, giving rise to greater mistrust among groups and increasing concern over past and current grievances among the groups. Declining job security and the opportunity for a better future for individuals and families has contributed to increased competition for scarce resources such as jobs and housing, creating a climate of suspicion and distrust of members of different racial, ethnic, and religious groups. It is probably also the basis for increased hostility toward recent immigrants, especially illegal immigrants, for allegedly taking the jobs or threatening the wages of other Americans.

Third, **Caring** is a combination of the desire to contribute to the well being of others and the opportunity to act on those desires. Caring may be expressed impersonally and indirectly, as in *checkbook caring*, or personally through face-to-face efforts to assist others. People who write checks to support groups that assist the homeless or the poor are an important part of the culture of giving.

Sometimes the importance of checkbook giving is dismissed as inauthentic or guilt-based; but what's wrong with guilt if it results in helping the less fortunate? Checkbook giving may at least reflect a recognition that people must assume some responsibility for the consequences of their action or inaction. Many people may have the desire to help others who are less fortunate, but they lack the resources of money or time to act on those desires.

In chapters 6 and 7 we focus attention on the declining opportunities for Americans to adequately care for the young, the next generation expected to carry the economic, political, and civic burdens of being productive members of society. With a growing number of American families being dual earners, there is a consequent decline in time available to parents to be with their children at home and in the community. Only families with sufficient financial resources can avoid being dual earners, or, if they are, can purchase quality child care or the cultural and educational experiences that contribute to better child development. In addition to the growing "time bind" of the contemporary family, there is the growing number of single-parent families that put their children at greater risk. Finally, there is the matter of the increasing importance of more and better education to give children a chance for better jobs and a more secure future. This leads us to examine the problem of parental involvement in their child's school activities and of large differences between resource-rich public schools and resource-poor public schools. Caring for the next generation must be linked to better schools for all children.

CYCLES OF HOPE, TRUST, AND CARING

One of the more interesting aspects of hope, trust, and caring is that they are interrelated. People who lack hope because of job loss or job insecurity are very unlikely to engage in behavior that reveals trust in other people or institutions or to have attitudes and behavior that reflect caring for others. Similarly, people who lack feelings of generalized trust are not very likely to exhibit caring behavior toward others who are not members of their in-group. And people who believe that they are "all alone out there" are not likely to be very sympathetic to the needs of others or to exhibit attitudes and behavior reflecting hope and trust. As a general principle of social life we may say that people who lack belief in a positive future or who believe that other people cannot be trusted or do not deserve caring are not likely to exhibit any of these positive qualities in their relations with others, or in their views of their social institutions.

Recognizing that hope, trust, and caring are interrelated is especially important when we start to think about remedies to improve the lives of Americans (chapter 8). For example, it may be technically and politically feasible to develop strategies to improve hope by expanding public employment opportunities. But if the policy excludes Americans who believe that they also are deserving of help, then hope will have been extended at the expense of trust; that is, loss of trust in a political system that helps some but not all who are deserving. Thus, when we begin to think about remedies in chapter 8, we will be mindful of the way that hope, trust, and caring can be part of an upward spiral of improvement, or a downward spiral of continued decline.

2

Job Loss and Declining Wages

In the spring of 2004, several months before the presidential election that pitted incumbent George W. Bush against John Kerry, a national poll reported that almost two-thirds of Americans expressed concern that they could lose their job because their employer might move that job to a foreign country. This poll happened to follow several high-profile articles in the *New York Times* and the *Wall Street Journal* about senior IBM officials discussing plans to move jobs in computer programming to foreign workers in China and India. This practice came to be labeled as "outsourcing" in the mainstream media, and some may have thought that the poll responses were influenced by the well-publicized comments by IBM officials. But the anxiety of the Americans answering the poll was probably also related to their awareness of the fact that some 2.8 million manufacturing jobs were lost between 2000 and 2003.[1] The average American would have to have been living in a cave not to be aware of what was happening to jobs of American workers, especially in manufacturing. And they weren't living in a cave, because when they were polled about the economy in 2007, only 27 percent of Americans rated the economy as "excellent" or "good," and 78 percent said the economy is "getting worse." When they were polled again in 2008 in a New York Times/CBS News poll, only 21 percent of the respondents said that the overall economy is in good shape.[2]

What were the economic and political forces that changed the state of manufacturing in the United States and made Americans so negative about their job situation? How is it that after World War II manufacturing made up 40 percent of the labor force, but in 2005 that share had slipped to 12 percent? Why is it that both Democratic and Republican candidates for the presidency in 2008 seemed to be clueless about what has happened to American jobs? The politicians may not want to know what happened because they played a central role in the demise of manufacturing, but the answers are there for anyone interested in knowing the answers. In this chapter we shall examine the American economy and what happened to the jobs and wages of the average American worker in two thirty-year periods: from post-WWII to 1975, and from 1975 to 2008.

POST–WORLD WAR II TO 1975: SOCIAL CONTRACT

In the early years following World War II, the United States was the dominant economic and military power among the industrialized nations of the world. This was due in large part to how and where the war was fought. In the years before the United States entered the war, industrial capacity was increased dramatically as the United States became the major supplier of military hardware to those nations already at war with Nazi Germany. But of greatest significance was the fact that the industrial nations of Europe—England, France, Italy, Germany, and the Soviet Union—were the battleground for the war. Not only did they suffer millions of military and civilian deaths but also their national industrial might and infrastructure was destroyed as a result of the air and ground assaults undertaken by both sides in the war. In the Far East, the once mighty industrial machine of the Japanese nation suffered greatly from the millions of tons of bombs dropped on the island, to say nothing of the effect of the two atomic bombs dropped on Hiroshima and Nagasaki.

These war-torn nations lost the factories that would produce the consumer goods for their people, and they lost a generation of young men and women who would make up the workforce they would need to do the work of rebuilding the nation. While the United States also suffered significant military deaths (about 450,000), the women and men in the civilian population were hard at work in the fields and factories producing food and military equipment. After the war the industrial capacity of the United States was shifted to the production of civilian goods. Many women who had been working full time and part time during the war left the labor force, but many remained to begin what would become a long-term trend of working women. Many returning veterans were reabsorbed into the labor force, but hundreds of thousands also used their GI benefits to enroll in colleges and universities throughout the nation.

The postwar experience of many Americans, both veterans and nonveterans, who embarked on new occupational careers and new educational pursuits laid the foundation for what was to become a generation who would build the American Dream of stable jobs, rising incomes, and home ownership. It is important to note that not all Americans were enjoying the new opportunities of the postwar world. Black Americans who were veterans also had the benefits of the GI Bill, but in the late 1940s, America was still a segregated society and black veterans could not attend most institutions of higher education. They could use their educational benefits to attend only historically black colleges that lacked the same diversity of programs and career opportunities that were available to the white GIs.

At the close of the war, there was concern that the U.S. economy could not sustain the high level of production, profits, and employment that was stimulated by war mobilization. The memory of the Great Depression and a fear that it might return, with its high level of unemployment and stagnation, led the United States to establish a new world economic system that would maintain its economic, political, and military dominance. The post-war geopolitical system of the United States was to provide extensive foreign assistance to the war-torn economies of Western Europe. The foreign assistance policy known as the Marshall Plan provided $22 billion in aid over a four-year period. This policy stimulated U.S. investment in Europe and provided the capital for European nations to buy U.S. agricultural and industrial products.

The dominance of American industry in the world economy was reflected in its role as the major exporter of goods and services to other nations, while importing very little from the rest of the world. This imbalance of exports versus imports was due to the previously mentioned devastating effects of the war on other industrialized countries. It would take years for the Japanese and European nations to rebuild their industrial capacity and to produce goods for their citizens and for export. In the meantime, the United States would dominate the world economy through its control of three-fourths of the world's investment capital and two-thirds of its industrial capacity.

The postwar system was the basis for U.S. growth and prosperity during the 1950s, the 1960s, and the early 1970s. This period of general economic expansion continued despite the Korean War in 1950–1953 and the U.S. war in Vietnam in 1965. This was also a period of strong union activity and the establishment of what became known as a "social contract" between management and organized labor. This informal agreement said that management would provide workers with stable wage increases, pensions, health insurance, and paid vacations; in return, workers provided high-productivity work performance, agreed-upon work rules, and minimal disruption of the workplace in the form of unauthorized strikes.

The clearest evidence that the social contract was working is the data on income growth for all income groups in the country. An examination of the income gains of each income quintile in the United States for the period

1949–1975 indicates that all income groups realized income growth, and that the highest rate of income growth was among the poorest 20 percent of Americans.[3] Clearly, these statistics indicate that economic growth during this period was a case of "a rising tide lifting all boats."

Some have argued that the gains of American workers during this period were won at a very high price. After a period of labor militancy reflected in local strikes and nationwide walkouts, a major labor-management accommodation was reached, which is described by Mike Davis as follows:

> The 1950 contract [between the UAW and General Motors] with its five-year no-strike pledge symbolized the end of the New Deal/Fair Deal cycle of class struggle and established the model of collective bargaining that prevailed until the 1980s. On the one side, the contract conceded the permanence of union representation and provided for the periodic increase of wages and benefits tied to productivity growth. On the other, the contract—by relinquishing worker protection against technological change, and by ensnaring grievance procedure in the bureaucratic maze—also liquidated precisely that concern for the rank-and-file power in the immediate labor process that had been the central axis for the 1933–37 upsurge in auto and mass production industries. As *Fortune* slyly put it at the time: GM may have paid a billion for the peace . . . It got a bargain.[4]

According to this critical view of the postwar social contract, organized labor became a major supporter of the postwar social order, and labor's commitment to businesslike collective bargaining left it ill-prepared for the impact of technology and global competition that it was to face in the 1970s.

FROM 1975 TO 1985: GLOBAL COMPETITION

The earliest warning sign indicating that the American economy was slowing down was found in the changing balance of economic power among industrialized nations. By the mid-1970s there was evidence of major improvements in the war-torn economies of Western Europe and Asia. The U.S. gross domestic product was three times as large as the Soviet Union's in 1950, but it declined to less than twice as large; it was less than four times the economy of Germany (down from nine times in 1950); and less than three times that of Japan (down from twelve times in 1950). As all these countries joined the United States in the production of goods for domestic consumption, it could be expected that the rate of economic growth in the United States would slow. The key questions were how much would it slow and what would corporate executives and elected government leaders do about it.

As annual corporate reports were released in the mid-1970s, it was clear that profits were in sharp decline; they went from an annual return of about 15 percent in the early 1960s to below 10 percent after 1975. The increase in global competition and the decline in corporate profits led to many discussions among corporate leaders, politicians, and the media about what went wrong and what could be done to change direction. The search for answers produced the following list of suspects.

1. In a version of blaming the victim, there was much discussion of the undue influence of organized labor that imposed heavy costs on corporations in the form of high-wage agreements and inflation-linked wage increases. There was also the claim that union control of work rules limited management's ability to try new production innovations to compete more effectively.
2. Another version of blaming the victim was the charge that American workers had become too secure and they therefore lacked the work ethic to compete in the global economy. American workers were often compared to Japanese workers who were held up as the icon of the committed worker.
3. The third suspect was the government with its new arsenal of regulations that imposed excessive costs on corporations and that tied the hands of management. Corporate executives complained about new workplace standards required by the Occupational Safety and Health Administration (OSHA), and air and water pollution standards required by the Environmental Protection Agency (EPA).

All of these criticisms laid the basis for attacks on organized labor and on workers' wages and for demands for relief from excessive government regulation. They also provided the justification for corporate decisions to close plants in the United States and move to low-wage countries with no unions and few regulations comparable to OSHA and EPA. They also led to expanded investment overseas, where profits from foreign investments greatly exceed profits from domestic investments.

What political leaders or the media rarely discussed was the failure of major U.S. corporations to respond to the increasing competition in the areas of autos, steel, textiles, and electronics. American corporations failed to follow the well-established management approach to competition, loss of market share, and declining profits, like investing in more efficient technology and research and development in support of product innovations. Instead of competing with foreign producers by strengthening the core industries of manufacturing—autos, steel, textiles, and consumer electronics—many of the largest U.S. multinationals embarked on a thirty-year frenzy of increased foreign investment, mergers and joint ventures with foreign firms, plant closings, downsizing the workforce, and outsourcing and offshoring domestic production. By 1981, the United States "was importing 26 percent of its cars, 25 percent of its steel, 60 percent of its televisions, tape recorders, radios, and phonographs, 43 percent of its calculators, 27 percent of its metal-forming machine tools, and 53 percent of its numerically controlled machine tools."[5] Imports from developing nations went from $3.6 billion in 1970 to $30 billion in 1980.

We now examine how changing global competition and the actions of corporations first impacted blue-collar workers, and later, white-collar workers.

PLANT CLOSINGS AND CAPITAL FLIGHT

On December 1, 1982, an RCA television cabinet factory in Monticello, Indiana, closed its doors and shut down production.[6] The town with its population of 5,000 people (the county had a population of 23,000) had been home to RCA since 1946, and many of its workers had been with the plant since the beginning. The 850 workers displaced by the closing were members of Local 3154 of the United Brotherhood of Carpenters and Joiners. The union had a successful record of negotiations with management on wage issues, pension contributions, health care costs, and work rules. But what can you do about a company that has decided to close its doors and move production to another country? In the American system of law, corporations have property rights, and they may choose to close down a plant in one location and rebuild it elsewhere. But workers do not have a right to their jobs in the RCA plant.

The initial response of workers was disbelief. Rumors of a plant closing were believed by some to be a management ploy to extract concessions from the union. But the company was not interested in negotiations; it simply stated that high manufacturing costs and foreign competition required movement of production elsewhere. Worker reactions to the closing were varied, ranging from despair and anger to confidence that they would find another job. Many of them were strengthened by the fact that they were solidly "middle class" workers who owned a home (along with the bank), had cars, recreational vehicles, small boats for fishing, and took vacations with their families.

What they didn't realize is that they were part of a decade-long rash of plant closings in a wide range of industries and that they would not be able to find another job in that same industry. What was disappearing was not just a plant or a job; an entire industry was either being eliminated or reorganized with a sharply reduced workforce. Between the late 1970s and the mid-1980s, more than 11 million workers lost their jobs because of plant shutdowns, relocation of facilities to other countries, or layoffs. The experiences of displaced workers were quite varied according to their sector of employment. Job loss was greatest for operators in manufacturing and those in mining and construction. Reemployment was highest among younger workers (<55) and lowest among workers who were displaced from jobs in manufacturing. When displaced workers found new jobs it was often in a sector with lower wages and no benefits and was often temporary or part-time employment. As we shall see in the next section, job loss among white-collar workers resulted in their own pattern of difficulties with reemployment.

During this decade of plant closings and worker displacement, direct investment abroad by U.S. corporations increased sharply. In 1970, direct investment abroad by U.S. firms was $75 billion, and it rose to $167 billion in 1978. In the 1980–1985 period, it remained below $400 billion, but it would continue to increase to a level of $716 billion by 1994. Foreign investment reached such high levels that by the mid-1990s the hundred largest multinational corporations would report anywhere from 30 percent to 68 percent of their total revenue from foreign sources.[7] American corporations were maintaining their profit margins by increased investment in affiliates abroad and by mergers and acquisitions, rather than investing in domestic production of autos, steel, and textile companies.

Building production facilities in foreign countries was made possible by extraordinary technological developments in computer-assisted design and manufacturing (CAD-CAM) and computer and satellite-based telecommunications systems. These innovations made it possible to have a spatially decentered firm, or a company that could produce a product with components manufactured in plants located in five or six other countries and then assembled at a single location for distribution and sale. The home headquarters of a global company could coordinate, via telecommunications, all the geographically dispersed activities of research, development, design, production, and sales decisions that go into making and selling a product. These innovations also made it possible for multinational firms to think about the existence of a global division of labor rather than being limited to workers in the home country.

Provisions in the corporate tax code also encouraged foreign investment by U.S. companies. Corporate profits made overseas are taxed at a lower rate than profits from domestic operations, and sometimes no taxes are paid until profits are returned to the United States. Thus, U.S. firms can amass significant profits and avoid taxes by continuing to reinvest their profits in overseas operations.

1985 TO 1995:
AUTO TRANSPLANTS, DOWNSIZING, AND NAFTA

Although corporations continued to move production abroad and to invest in overseas operations, two major events in this decade would have significant impact on American workers. The first event was the competition among states and communities that were hard hit by plant closings and substantial job losses to try to attract new companies and jobs. Several of the so-called Rust Belt states like Michigan, Ohio, and Illinois were drawn into competing to attract new industry, and the big prize at the time was Japanese auto assembly plants.[8] The 1980s was a time when the number of imports of Toyota and Honda cars was expanding and was having a significant impact on the sales of autos produced by the Big Three (GM, Ford, and Chrysler). The White House and Congress were considering establishing quotas on the number of autos imported into the United States, but there was concern that this form of protectionism might lead to a trade war between the United States and Japan. An alternative idea was to encourage the Japanese to build auto plants in the United States and produce cars for the domestic market. The Japanese liked this idea because they feared that Congress might set quotas on imports under pressure from the Big Three and the United Auto Workers union that had experienced major job losses in the auto industry. The Big Three and the UAW liked the idea because they thought this would level the playing field between the Japanese and American auto manufacturers. American auto executives and union leaders believed that the Japanese production efficiencies in Japan were the result of having a workforce that was more easily intimidated by their management and more willing to accept work rules and work pressure that American workers would never accept. American auto executives also believed that when the Japanese had to build cars with American workers and pay U.S. wages and benefits, they would no longer have a competitive advantage. What American leaders failed to understand is that Japanese production methods were able to produce higher quality cars with long-term reliability and that these methods would be brought to and applied in the United States.

So the Japanese said "yes," they were willing to build auto assembly plants in the United States, and the competition began in earnest among the states to get Toyota, Honda, Nissan, Mitsubishi, and Subaru-Isuzu to choose them for their plant site. And how did they compete? They did so by offering Japanese companies "incentive packages" filled with taxpayer subsidized "goodies" like preparation of the land site with road improvements and utilities, property tax waivers, worker training costs, and even funds for special educational programs for the children of Japanese executives. The state of Kentucky, for example, provided Toyota with about $200 million in incentives, including $12.5 million for purchase of land, $20 million to prepare the land for site plant construction, $47 million for road improvements, $65 million for worker training, and $5.2 million for special educational needs of Japanese families.

The Toyota-Kentucky incentive package was repeated with local variations in Ohio (Honda), Michigan (Mazda), Illinois (Mitsubishi), Tennessee (Nissan), and Indiana (Subaru-Isuzu). A total of more than 1 billion "incentive package" dollars was put up front to secure Japanese auto plants in six Midwest states. For the 1,000 to 2,000 workers who would be hired to work in these new plants, the money for the incentives would seem like money well spent. And it would certainly be seen as a good idea for the business community that benefits from growth, especially the banks, lawyers, land developers, and realtors who would facilitate the new growth-related business that would follow the transplanted company.

Obviously, there are economic benefits associated with growth, but benefits for whom? Nobody asked the people in the communities where the Japanese plants located whether they thought that it was a "good deal" to spend more than $50,000 of taxpayers' money for each new job that would be created. No one asked the local citizens if they would prefer to spend the tax dollars in different ways, such as helping local small businesses to start up and expand or to provide tax incentives to start up U.S. companies.

You are probably thinking, what difference does it make if the 2,000 new workers are working for the Japanese or American companies? It makes a difference that the Japanese plants are not union plants. It makes a difference that the Japanese plants pay about one-half the wage-benefit package as U.S. unionized auto plants. This puts downward pressure on all wages in a region and undercuts efforts to unionize workers in any industry. Yes, union plants force employers to pay more in wages and benefits, which is why strong unions help build a middle class with job security and wage increases. An additional difference is that a foreign company does not produce the entire vehicle in the United States. A GM plant is more likely to produce the entire vehicle—body, transmission, electronics, etc.—in the United States, but the Japanese produce their high-value-added components like the drive train and electronics in Japan. This means that General Motors employs more highly paid and skilled engineers, designers, and technical professionals in the United States to produce their cars, while the Japanese employ mainly lower-wage auto assembly workers. Finally, the Japanese firms take their profits back to Japan for further investment, while GM invests its profits, if it ever makes any, in the United States.

The end result of this effort to "level the playing field" by requiring the Japanese to build plants in the United States was a steady decline in the sale of autos produced by GM, Ford, and Chrysler and growth of the share of the auto market going to Japanese auto firms. By 2007, Toyota would, for the first time in auto sales history, sell more cars than were sold by General Motors. As the U.S. auto industry continued to lose market share, it would respond by cutting jobs held by the still unionized, but much smaller, United Auto Workers and moving production to lower-wage areas.

The second major event affecting American workers between 1985 and 1995 was the practice of "downsizing," or slimming down the workforce in order to save money. After a decade of success (1975–1985) in closing U.S. plants, shifting production and investment abroad, and cutting both labor and labor costs (both the number of production workers and wage-benefit packages), major corporations now turned their attention to saving money by cutting white-collar employees. When Sears, Roebuck and Company announced that it would cut 50,000 jobs in the 1990s, the value of its stock increased, to the delight of Sears's stockholders. Cutting jobs and reducing waste became the new way companies would become "lean and mean" and improve their profit margins. Every month seemed to carry a new downsizing decision: Tenneco Incorporated would cut 11,000 of its 29,000 employees; Delta Airlines would cut 18,800 jobs; Eastman Kodak chipped in 16,800 cuts; AT&T announced 40,000 cuts; and IBM got into the game with an announcement that it would cut 180,000 jobs between 1987 and 1994.

Not to be outdone, even the upscale financial sector joined in with downsizing plans. A rash of bank mergers resulted in new "efficiencies," meaning that they would reduce payrolls. For example, when Chase Manhattan Bank acquired Chemical Banking Corporation in a merger, both banks announced job cuts of 12,000 employees. The downsizing bandwagon was fed by a desire for real efficiencies and by the need to show stockholders that management was serious about eliminating "fat" and waste.

Downsizing took its greatest toll on better-educated and better-paid workers who were classified as middle managers and supervisors. Just as blue-collar workers felt the impact of new production technology in the 1975–1985 decade, white-collar workers found themselves replaced by new computer-based data management systems and computer-based surveillance systems that could oversee clerical workers and data-entry workers. The new technology increased overall productivity without adding more employees.

The downsizing efforts of this decade, combined with the job losses in manufacturing in the previous decade, led to a new way that corporations began to think about their employees. Some workers were viewed as part of the "core," meaning that they possessed the skills, knowledge, and experience that were essential to profit-producing operations of the company. Being in the core is not the same as being in an occupational group; for example, some engineers will be in the core and some will not. Some departments are in the core, and some are not. For example, the human relations department is important in a company, but it does not contribute to core functions that lead to profits. If a plant must cut costs, it is more likely to look for savings in human relations than in production or sales. Being in the core means that the work performed is essential to the profit-producing functions of the firm. The job security of core workers is linked to the existence of a group of "temporary workers" who are hired and released according to product demands and sales. The company not only makes no commitment to "temps" but also it may have a different wage and benefit package for them.

The Japanese auto plants in the Midwest that we discussed above also made effective use of differentiating between core and temporary employees. For example, an auto plant with 2,000 production workers would make "no layoff" commitments to 1,200 "core" workers and then hire 800 temporary workers through a national temporary worker agency like Manpower, Inc. If sales decline and auto inventories increase, the temporary workers are laid off while the core workers remain.

Joining the "core" and "temp" workers are "contingent workers," who are a mix of part-time employees and independent contractors. Contingent workers are usually hired through a temp agency and they may include production workers, clerical, engineers, computer specialists, and lawyers. They are usually employees of the temp agency that contracts them to companies for short-term, specific jobs. Contingent workers and temp workers probably harbor the hope that the company will recognize their value and will keep them in permanent positions. This often leads such workers to be "overperformers" and unintentionally serve as a means to intimidate core workers to give their best.

The final "nail in the coffin" of lost working-class jobs was the North American Free Trade Agreement (NAFTA) in 1993. This legislation, which was supported by President Bill Clinton and a majority of both houses of Congress, was championed by political leaders as leading to "free trade" between the United States, Mexico, and Canada and as creating more jobs in the United States because of a growth in U.S. exports. Unfortunately, the main thing that was exported was more U.S. jobs to Mexico. NAFTA also allowed for the creation of Export Processing Zones (EPZ) in Mexico right across the border from the United States. The plants that were built in the zone were called maquiladora plants, and they were given very favorable tax agreements in return for producing goods that were for export only.

It is worth remembering that in the 1992 presidential election that pitted Bill Clinton against George H. W. Bush, there was a third-party candidate named Ross Perot who was very concerned about U.S. companies shipping jobs overseas. One of his favorite lines in his campaign speeches was to refer to the "giant sucking sound of jobs leaving the country." The corporate elite and the political elite were not happy with Perot's message, and the mainstream media helped the elite's "free trade" agenda by giving Perot the persona of a quirky, eccentric millionaire who was trying to buy the presidency because he had nothing better to do with his money. Perot was eccentric, and he was a millionaire, but he also had a message that many Americans heard. In the 1992 election Perot received an astounding 19 percent of the popular vote, which is unheard of for a third-party candidate in a presidential election. What Ross Perot achieved with his presidential run was not a change in U.S. trade policies but probably the election of Bill Clinton, because many of the votes that Perot received probably would have gone to Bush. Perot was undoubtedly correct about the "giant sucking sound," because economists estimate that in the years 1994 to 2003, NAFTA led to the loss of over 900,000 U.S. jobs to Mexico.[9]

Although millions of jobs were lost due to plant closings in 1975 to 1985 and downsizing and NAFTA in 1985 to 1995, this fact was often hidden from public view by the media because of the steady growth of new jobs during the latter part of the 1990s. One of the frequently mentioned achievements of President Clinton's second term was job growth and the historically low unemployment rate. However, what was rarely mentioned was the fact that most of the jobs that were created were in the low-wage, no-benefits service sector that were hardly comparable to the wages and benefits of the manufacturing jobs that were shipped overseas. And as for the low unemployment of 4.3 percent, as with every unemployment rate it failed to report on part-time workers who want full-time work or on discouraged workers who have stopped looking. If these workers were added to the mix, the 4.2 percent unemployment rate would be 7.5 percent.[10]

1995 TO 2008: OUTSOURCING JOBS OFFSHORE

The final arrow in the corporate quiver of how to reduce jobs and wage costs is "outsourcing," and it surfaced as a prominent strategy in the last decade. Outsourcing was facilitated by the Internet, which made it possible for computer-mediated tasks to be conducted by persons in many different geographical locations. The type of work that is most frequently outsourced is that done primarily in customer service call centers and work by skilled programmers.[11] Outsourced call centers are especially attractive in India, where college-educated, English-speaking young women and men can be employed for a fraction of comparable U.S. costs.

The interest in Internet-linked programmers from India, China, or Eastern Europe is based on a belief in the high quality of their computer training, and especially in the wage comparison between the countries. One estimate places the cost of a programmer in the United States at $80,000 a year on average, compared with $20,000 or less in India.[12] However, it should be recognized that the decision to outsource the technical work of engineers or programmers is based on more than wage differential. Some projects require face-to-face meetings, and Internet-linked programmers or engineers may not be the best choice. Finally, wage differentials may not be large enough to offset the costs of building a new facility in China or India, in transportation costs for supplies or completed products, or in the availability of parts suppliers for certain products.

Many companies also outsourced work without sending the jobs overseas. For example, suppose an IBM facility has a maintenance department that is responsible for cleaning and upgrading physical facilities like offices, lunchrooms, meeting rooms, and restrooms. As employees in the maintenance department they probably are eligible for the same benefit package as other employees. If, however, IBM chooses to outsource the maintenance functions to XYZ Cleaners, it can eliminate this group of employees and avoid paying their social security and any other benefits. Even if the number of employees remains the same, the wage-benefit level and job security of XYZ employees might not be comparable to what they had at IBM. A great many large companies have probably outsourced jobs to other companies within the United States, but detailed data on such practices are hard to obtain.

THIRTY YEARS OF JOB LOSS
AND DECLINING WAGES: CONSEQUENCES

The result of over three decades of plant closings, shifting investment abroad, downsizing, and outsourcing by America's largest and most well-known corporations has had both intended and unintended consequences. The intended consequence was to increase profits, increase productivity, and to remain competitive. Each individual corporation did what it thought was rational for the company and its shareholders. But the combined consequences of these individually rational corporate decisions produced the profound unintended consequence of dramatically shrinking the middle class in America. The erosion of middle-class jobs with good wages, security, and benefits left in its place a society made up of a privileged class of owners, corporate executives, managers, and professionals (20 percent of Americans), a shrinking class of skilled, middle-income workers (20 percent), and a new working class of Americans (60 percent) with fewer skills, insecure jobs, low wages, and no pensions or health insurance.

Table 2.1 provides a picture of how the economic class structure of the United States has changed over the last thirty years. The table divides the population of the United States into five quintile groups ranging from the top 20 percent to the bottom 20 percent and reports the share of national income received by each quintile group in 1974 and 2004.[13]

Table 2.1.　Share of National Income by Quintiles of Population

	1974	2004	Percent Change in Shares
Top 20%	40.6	47.9	+18%
Second 20%	24.1	23.0	− 3%
Third 20%	17.6	15.4	−11%
Fourth 20%	12.0	9.6	−19%
Bottom 20%	5.7	4.0	−26%

The top 20 percent received almost half (47.9 percent) of national income in 2004, and the second 20 percent received a little more than its share (23 percent). All other income groups received less than their share of national income. Only one group, the top 20 percent, experienced an increase in their share of national income (18 percent) while the other four groups experienced declines ranging from a loss of 3 percent to a loss of 26 percent.

Thirty years of job loss and wage stagnation have produced a high level of income inequality and wealth inequality between the top 20 percent of Americans and everyone else. Finally, it produced trade deficits at historic levels, making the United States a debtor nation, because we import more goods from the rest of the world than we export to them. The value of imports from other nations was $3.6 billion in 1970. By 2004, the deficit reached a record high of $617.7 billion; $75.2 deficit with Japan, $162 billion with China, $45.1 billion with Mexico, $68.5 billion with Canada, and $110 billion with the European Union. Multinational corporations in the United States that had built plants and invested overseas were the big winners from this trade deficit because they were producing goods made by low-wage foreign workers and shipping them back for sale in America. And they did it with the full approval and support of several presidents and members of several Congresses with bipartisan support.

Discussion of trade deficits is usually presented to suggest that the United States is importing goods from other countries like Mexico or China and that we are competing with foreign producers of products for American consumers. That is true in part, but it doesn't tell the entire story. The calculation of trade deficits identifies the geographic source of imports, not the ownership of the company that is producing the imported products. So, the $162 billion of imports from China in 2004 actually includes imports from U.S.-owned firms that are producing goods in China and exporting them to the United States. The U.S. Department of Commerce reports that 47 percent of consumption imports were "related party trade," which means "trade by U.S. companies with their subsidiaries abroad as well as trade with U.S. subsidiaries of foreign companies with their parent companies."[14]

Thus, a major part of our trade deficit comes from U.S. companies producing goods in other countries and exporting them for their subsidiaries or for U.S. consumers. As the comic strip character Pogo once said, "We have met the enemy and it is us."

Most members of the privileged class benefited greatly from the global economy and the actions of multinational firms to increase profits by investing and producing in countries other than the United States. The average American also was supposed to have benefited from foreign imports because the products that were imported and sold in the big retail stores like Wal-Mart cost less, and it kept the cost of living for Americans low. However, what the new working class received was greater job insecurity, reduced wages and salaries, fewer benefits in the form of pensions and health insurance, and no prospect that things might improve in the future. Do you think the average American would rather have a secure job with good wages or a sweatshirt that costs less than if it was produced in a textile mill by American workers in South Carolina?

We now describe this new class structure in more detail, because it is essential to an understanding of how events in the last thirty-plus years in America led to a decline of hope, trust, and caring, which we believe are essential for a healthy individual and a healthy society. In America today, the class position of a family is based primarily on income, wealth, and education, especially the source of education. Occupation is also important, but entry into high-paying occupations is usually linked to higher education, and one's occupation is worth a whole lot more if you obtain your training from an elite school such as Yale, or Princeton, or Harvard, rather than an obscure state college or university.[15] For example, if your law degree is from an elite university you are more likely to become employed in a national law firm with a six-figure salary.[16] People with high incomes, accumulated assets, and a quality education are likely to be members of the "privileged class." They are in the privileged class because they have stable and secure resources that are found in four types of capital: *consumption capital*, or income; *investment capital*, or stocks, bonds, and savings; *skill capital*, or specialized training attained through experience or education; and *social capital*, or networks of family, friends, and school-related ties. This class contains about 1 to 2 percent of the population who are owners of large businesses, earning six- and seven-figure incomes. It also includes about 13 to 15 percent who are mid- and upper-level managers and CEOs of corporations and public organizations, who also have six- and seven-figure salaries. And there are about 4 to 5 percent who are doctors, lawyers, academics at elite universities, and finance analysts with credentials from highly ranked colleges and professional schools. Altogether, people in this class account for about 20 percent of Americans, and they all have incomes ranging from $100,000 a year to upper six figures (in 1969 only 4 percent of Americans had incomes in excess of $100,000). In 2004, the total income of this top 20 percent (top quintile) of Americans accounted for almost 48 percent of all income. This means that the total value of income earned by the top quintile of Americans was about equal to the total income earned by the remaining 80 percent of Americans.[17] While members of the privileged class are similar because of their substantial economic resources, they may be more heterogeneous on cultural values and their views on social issues like abortion, gun ownership, or the death penalty.

While this privileged class was growing in numbers and accumulating more income and wealth, middle-income Americans—the "middle class"—were declining. In 1969, middle-income Americans ($25,000 to $49,999 a year) made up 41 percent of the population, but that number declined to 27.2 percent in 2002.

Members of the privileged class also control a great deal of wealth, and the degree of wealth inequality is far greater than income inequality. Wealth is the total value of what people own, such as stocks, bonds, 401(k) accounts at work, and homes, minus debt such as mortgages, car loans, and credit cards. In 2001, the top quintile of Americans held 66 percent of total wealth (financial assets plus real estate), while the bottom four quintiles (80 percent) had 33 percent of wealth. If you exclude real estate and look only at financial assets (stocks, bonds, etc.), the top quintile controls 93 percent of financial wealth and the remaining 80 percent of Americans control 7 percent.[18] The reason for the big difference between total wealth and financial assets is that the wealth of most Americans is contained in the value of their homes.

Middle-income, working-class Americans (20 percent of the population) are not entirely homogeneous when it comes to income or their social and cultural beliefs. At the top of this class are skilled workers like nurses, schoolteachers, civil servants, carpenters, machinists, electricians, and owners of very small businesses. Their incomes are usually between $35,000 and $50,000 (a $20-per-hour job yields $40,000 a year) and some may earn more because of overtime opportunities. Some in this group may have a higher family income ($60,000 to $70,000 a year) because many are dual earners, with a spouse who has a part-time or full-time job. Some in this group may still have the protection of a union contract, but what they all have as their source of security is that there is a labor market for their skill. For example, nurses may have more security than machinists because health care is more difficult to outsource. But security for all in this group is tenuous because we know that many skilled jobs in the 1980s and 1990s were lost due to new technology that displaced workers or made it possible for less-skilled workers to do their jobs. Since the skill is embedded in the new technology rather than in accumulated work experience, these jobs can always be outsourced to less-educated and less-skilled workers in low-wage countries.

Located just below skilled workers are the vast number of less-educated and less-skilled wage earners in clerical and sales jobs, personal services, transportation, food services, and machine operators and assemblers. They make up about 60 percent of the workforce. Members of this group are high school graduates and dropouts, and increasingly, graduates of community colleges or four-year colleges who are unable to find better job opportunities and have been forced into the lower-wage earner group. Incomes for wage earners are in the minimum wage to $15 per hour range ($20,000 to $35,000 per year).

Very few members of the middle- and lower-income groups in the working class have anything resembling wealth. A few have a defined-benefit pension plan that is provided by the employer, but these pension plans are a thing of the past and rarely found in today's workplace. The most successful may have been able to buy a home, but they probably still have a mortgage. Some may have enough discretionary income, or have a working spouse, to have started a 401(k), but most accounts will have modest assets.[19] Only the most affluent Americans have enough surplus income to amass enough savings in such accounts to enable them to accumulate wealth over their life span. They are members of the working class because they have limited and insecure resources found in their income, investments and savings, credentialed skill or education, and social connections.

The experience of working-class Americans over the last thirty years has been like a dagger thrust into the heart of hope. The erosion of hope started with the wave of plant closings that began in the late 1970s, and workers who were caught up in this dramatic shift away from the post–World War II "social contract" could hardly comprehend what was happening. After working for the same company for years they woke up one morning to find out that the company was gone, that it "moved." Workers may lose their jobs, and companies sometimes went out of business, but they didn't just up and move. There is a difference between a situation where some workers are losing their jobs when the company is still operating and all workers losing their jobs because the plant has closed and moved operations overseas. The reactions of the first wave of displaced workers that we interviewed in the early 1980s reveal responses that capture exactly what we mean by the loss of hope, trust, and caring. Consider the following comments of a twenty-six-year-old divorced woman reflecting upon her experience with becoming a displaced worker following a plant closing.[20]

I have taken a lot of jobs since I lost my job at RCA. And I have found that there is little I can do for the experience and education I have. Waitressing is not my lifelong dream but I can find a job in that field better than any other, so I have to do what I have to do. I have no benefits and future and no light at the end of the tunnel. You survive and grow old with nothing to show except varicose veins and a smile from those who say "girl get me this" and "I thought you went home you took so long." Only four or five tables who want your undivided attention at the same time. And a government that gets 8 percent of the meager $2.00 per hour I get.

And a comment by a forty-five-year-old married man.

We are down to rock bottom and will probably have to sell the house to live or exist until I find a job here or somewhere else. I have been everywhere looking in Cass, White and Carroll counties. We have had no help at anytime except when NIPSCO was going to shut the utilities off in March and the trustee paid that $141. My sister-in-law helps us sometime with money she's saved back or with food she canned last summer. The factories have the young. I've been to all the factories.

These two displaced workers are pretty much running on empty when it comes to hope. But the effect of losing your job in a plant closing extends beyond a loss of hope; it also involves a loss of trust in basic social institutions and extreme cynicism about other people. Consider the following comment by a thirty-two-year-old married woman who was displaced by a plant closing.

I personally believe that our country's problems lay with the dishonest persons. From the man drawing a paycheck without service given, to lawyers and Congress holding things up, stretching them out, which takes big dollars from people and business. There seems to be 1,001 middlemen in business and government and unions causing outstanding overhead. Agencies, like welfare, so big they lost track of people. They play with paper and machines and we are getting ripped off. The good old lying, cheating, drug-drunk bug is what is killing our country.

And another comment by a thirty-nine-year-old married female displaced worker.

I find that working for a company that kicks my backside out the door makes me afraid to trust anyone. I'm afraid it will be years before I get up the courage to buy a car, appliances, or anything that is on a long-term note. Regardless of how good the pay is in a new job. If we all managed our homes the way the government manages theirs we'd all be on welfare. I have a National Honor Society daughter with one more year of school. If she can't get aid there's no way she can go to school.

Anger is also among the responses of displaced workers, and one can see the roots of using stereotypes and scapegoats as a way of dealing with their frustration. Consider the following comment by a forty-one-year-old married man who was displaced by a plant closing.

The government is trying to cut our wages and put their foot in the working class and poor class face. Yet they keep raising their wages and find more ways than necessary to spend the taxpayer's money. Let the utility, telephone, and petroleum corporations, also the big money boys have their own way without fighting for the behalf of all people of our country. They also let the illegal aliens take our jobs away, give them welfare, unemployment compensation, college education at our expense; do not check them for health and social diseases. Yet they want to take all the veteran's benefits away from those who fought their wars for them. Government of the people, by the people, and for the people—Ha!

The loss of hope and despair expressed by these blue-collar workers who lost their jobs when their plant closed and moved to another country would be duplicated by white-collar workers confronted by downsizing in the 1990s. During the downsizing wave of the early 1990s, millions of older, better-educated, and better-paid middle managers would lose their jobs because of mergers, technological efficiencies, and cost cutting. Consider the case of an operations manager for a plant in San Fernando Valley.

[He] lost his $130,000-a-year job in January 1993 when the plant he managed was shut down permanently. After giving twenty-six years of his life and loyalty to one big corporation, Eastman Kodak, he found himself chasing white-collar jobs in a market already glutted with unemployed manufacturing executives.[21]

This former manager is lucky compared to displaced blue-collar workers, because his family survives on savings put away during the good times. His optimism has been shaken ("I believe in the American Dream. I feel it fading."), and he expresses concern that his wife and children will think less of him: "I know I'll never feel safe again. I lost my job, I failed my family."[22]

Oddly enough, the erosion of trust and caring extends to those who deliver the bad news when downsizing occurs ("the executioners"). They describe how they are affected by their role in their former co-workers' misfortune.

At first, it hurt in the stomach in the morning. It may seem callous, but after a while there's a sort of numbing. You go through the steps without getting too emotional. And you think to yourself, "When will my day come to be on the other side of the desk?"[23]

As we pointed out at the end of chapter 1, it is difficult to be caring about the plight of those in trouble when you are also operating in a climate of fear about Who's next?

This chapter is the first step in our journey to document the decline of hope, trust, and caring. In chapter 3 we consider the American Dream and the experiences of Americans from three different age groups related to the promise of the Dream.

3

The American Dream Is Fading

The American Dream is a set of beliefs that provides an idealized image of the life that an average person can live in America. The Dream is made up of four key beliefs. First is a belief that Americans should have a secure job that provides enough income to cover their basic needs. Second is a belief that through hard work and careful savings any American should be able to become a home owner. Third is a belief that there is equal opportunity for every American to reach his or her maximum potential. Fourth, that children in the average American family will have the opportunity to exceed the attainments of their parents. When the Dream becomes a reality for a great many Americans, as it did for the post–World War II generation, you have the ingredients of a middle-class society. This doesn't mean that all are able to live the Dream but that all will have the chance to do so, and many actually do so.

As we learned from chapter 2, about one in five Americans (20 percent) are living the American Dream to the fullest extent; they are in the privileged class and for them it is the Dream on steroids. They have enough accumulated wealth for their long-term security, and their incomes are sufficient to cover not only basic needs but also all sorts of creature comforts associated with expensive homes, cars, vacations, and consumption at a level once reserved only for royalty. Moreover, their incomes permit them to provide their daughters and sons with so many advantages that they will easily be able to join their parents in the privileged class. The other 80 percent of Americans are in the middle- and low-income brackets and they find that their jobs are increasingly insecure, that their incomes barely keep up with inflation, and that owning a home, a car, and big-ticket household luxuries may be slipping away as realistic aspirations. More importantly, the opportunity to achieve one's personal version of the good life, or the American Dream, may no longer exist for the average American, or for their children.

Even today, at the time of this writing, Americans have a dim view of their situation. An April 2008 poll conducted by the Pew Research Center asked Americans the following question: "Compared with five years ago, is it more or less difficult for middle-class people to maintain their standard of living?" The middle-class respondents were those earning between $40,000 and $100,000, and 78 percent of them said they were having a more difficult time. If these Americans who are earning above the median income for all Americans are having a more difficult time in the last five years, what would Americans with earnings below the median income say? About 25 percent of all respondents said their economic situation had not improved, and almost one-third said that they had actually fallen backwards. The future does not look any brighter for those in the Pew survey, in that about half of middle-class respondents said they expected to have to cut back on spending in the years ahead and about 25 percent said they were worried that they might be laid off, that their job would be outsourced, or that their employer would relocate in the coming year.

There is also some evidence that black Americans have become more discouraged about whether the American Dream applies to their race. Although the African American middle class has grown from the 1960s to the present, its members have started to question the likelihood of realizing the American Dream.[1]

Most Americans are aware that the ideal of the Dream always confronts the reality of existing inequality. They are aware that some young women and men start out life enjoying the Dream. As the old baseball joke goes, "they woke up on third base and thought they hit a triple," meaning that they had the good fortune to have had parents with good jobs and incomes while they were growing up. They are aware that they live in a stratified society made up of different occupational groups and different income groups. Although it has been that way since the beginning of industrialized America, people have always held the belief that the social position a person has at birth does not have to become one's destiny. People may improve their occupational and economic conditions through their own efforts because of the existence of established pathways of upward mobility. The belief and the reality was that improvement could come within a generation, or certainly across generations. A family could start a small business in their neighborhood, usually an ethnic niche, and provide a better life for themselves and their children. Family businesses were started and grew and were often inherited by their children. If children wanted something more than working in a family business, much to the disappointment of the parents, that son or daughter could go to college and be exposed to numerous new opportunities.

The opportunity for upward mobility was available to the second and third generations of ethnic Americans who benefited from the struggles of their parents' immigrant generation during the early decades of the twentieth century. Many, but not most, sons and daughters of Italian, Irish, Jewish, and Greek immigrants became skilled workers through union-sponsored apprentice programs; many started their own small business; and many went to college to become teachers and social workers, and sometimes doctors and lawyers. There was enough upward mobility by ethnic sons and daughters to support a general belief in the reality of the Dream. Probably every ethnic family in the early decades of the twentieth century had at least one member of the kin group who "made it out." After World War II, a belief in the ideals and reality of the Dream was expanded by the experiences of the returning veterans who used their GI benefits to go to college and move up the occupational ladder.

African Americans were rarely participants in the Dream during the early part of the twentieth century. They were living in a very segregated society with limited educational opportunities and little chance to get into skilled trade jobs. Unions were not very sympathetic to the desires of black workers to become stonemasons or machinists or carpenters. There were a small number of black professionals who received their education in historically black colleges, and sometimes they received their advanced professional degrees in white medical schools and law schools. But this advanced education was often provided with the understanding that the new doctor or lawyer would return to the black community to practice their profession. As we noted in chapter 1, even black veterans of World War II could not take full advantage of the GI Bill because most institutions of higher education were segregated.

THE AMERICAN DREAM AND PAST GENERATIONS

The possibility of realizing the Dream continued throughout the 1950s and 1960s, for reasons that were unique to that time but would be difficult to reproduce today. Let us try to use a personal story of the first author that provides anecdotal evidence of the reality of the Dream in past decades. He was the only child of an Italian-born father who came to this country when he was nine years of age and an American-born mother who had Italian immigrant parents. The father had a sixth-grade education and worked as a construction laborer in the 1930s and as a taxi cab driver for thirty-five years (he never was able to own his own cab because he never accumulated enough money to buy a medallion—the license of ownership). The mother claimed to have a high school diploma, and she worked as a domestic in the 1940s and then for forty years as a clerk in a neighborhood dry cleaning store. Their son had a good academic record in the primary grades and eventually tested his way into a science-oriented high school that admitted students from across the city based on scores on a competitive entrance exam. The son never thought of himself as having embarked on the Dream. In fact, he regretted his decision to attend the prestigious high school because it took him away from all his neighborhood buddies who went to the same nearby high school. His grades were low, and he was so unhappy at his special high school that in his senior year he simply quit and went to work as a new-car mechanic in an Oldsmobile dealership and then as a construction worker in the newly created Levittown on Long Island. In 1951 he was drafted into the U.S. Marine Corps and served until 1953. When he was discharged he used his Korean War benefits to get his high school diploma in a night school for dropouts and then enrolled in an obscure state teachers college (probably the only place that would accept his weak high school record; no SATs required) with the goal of becoming an elementary school teacher. His GI benefits provided $90 a month for four years (equivalent to about $500 per month today), but no money for tuition or for book expenses. It may be worth noting that WWII benefits provided a monthly stipend for four years, full tuition, and book expenses. I wonder why the politicians were so much more generous to WWII vets compared to Korean War vets? The tuition difference didn't matter much, since his college tuition was only $18 a semester. To make a long story short, his performance in college was exceptional, leading several of his professors to push him into graduate school. He eventually obtained a PhD in sociology and became a professor at a very good state university.

A second personal anecdote from the life of the second author reveals how unplanned intervention by forces beyond one's control shape the life course in ways that are consistent with the American Dream. She grew up in a small town in the mid-South. Her performance in elementary and high school indicated that she was an exceptional student. She definitely planned to attend college and could easily have been admitted to an elite private university in the state or to the state's major public university. But her family could not afford the cost of tuition and room and board to live away from home. So she enrolled in the regional public university that was located in her hometown and lived at home. Once again, her performance in college put her near the top of her class, but she had no plans for post-graduate education because of the costs associated with such a decision. But fate interceded. In 1957, the Soviet Union shocked the world by launching a satellite into space. The Soviet *Sputnik* circling the earth pushed the United States into a rapid-response catch-up program. The government established the National Defense Education Act, which was designed to support graduate education for the nation's best undergraduates by paying tuition and providing a fellowship to cover four years of graduate education. So, our second author was awarded an NDEA fellowship, which she used to obtain a PhD in sociology and embark on an academic career.

The personal anecdote of the first author is a good example of the Dream at its best; someone who starts life at the bottom, makes lots of bad decisions early in life like dropping out of high school, yet is still able to get a second chance at going to college and entering a rewarding occupation with high standing, security, and a good income. The personal anecdote of the second author reveals the powerful role that the federal government can play in providing opportunities for talented students with limited financial means. The point of these stories is to make the argument that although the Dream once worked, it probably could not be reproduced today. And why is that? First, although the system of class inequality in the 1950s and 1960s still made life difficult for people in the working class, that class structure was more open to those who made the effort to improve their social and economic positions. College was not the be-all and end-all for many young people because there were still opportunities for people to become skilled machinists or bricklayers or electricians; those were desirable and respected occupations that provided rewarding work, respect, and material benefits. A high school graduate would face a difficult choice deciding whether to take a union job in an auto plant or a steel mill or go to college. A good union job often provided better salaries and benefits than one might get as a primary or secondary schoolteacher or a social worker. For those who wanted college, the choice of going to college after high school was also a more realistic choice, because college education was the main avenue for significant upward mobility, and it was more available in two respects. First, since the number of people with high school diplomas was smaller, and the number seeking college admission was much smaller than today, public colleges and universities did not have the same requirements for admission such as Scholastic Aptitude Test exam scores (SAT), and therefore they relied more on high school performance records. The use of specialized exams for those seeking admission to professional schools in law, medicine, or business has also become a more standard requirement. Second, college tuition was also much more affordable for students and families in the 1950s and 1960s. Many students in large urban areas attended city colleges and paid very low tuition. They often continued to live at home, thereby avoiding the housing and food costs of living away from home. The main cost of going to college for such students was the forgone income associated with going to college and not taking a full-time job. In contrast, college attendance today might entail at minimum about $20,000 a year for tuition, room and board, books, and related expenses, and a maximum of $45,000 a year. A family earning $60,000 a year, which is above the median income in the United States, could hardly afford an annual expense equal to one-third or two-thirds of their income.

THE AMERICAN DREAM TODAY

The class structure in post-1975 America became much more rigid, making it more difficult for people to achieve upward mobility by getting better jobs or attaining more education. The disappearance of high-wage jobs in manufacturing limited the opportunity for people to move up the occupational ladder. Chances for upward mobility were also limited by increasing inequality in education available to children from modest- and lower-income groups. Primary and secondary schools became more stratified into resource-rich schools in the suburbs and resource-poor schools in the central cities, producing very unequal educational experiences for children born into privileged families compared to those from working-class families. Finally, higher education became highly stratified, with sharp distinctions made between elite colleges and universities, nonelite state schools, and community colleges. In contrast, in the 1960s and 1970s, having obtained a college degree by itself was enough of an advantage in the job market.

In this chapter we will do two things. First, we will examine evidence of whether the economic conditions of workers declined after 1975, leading to a decline in their income and standard of living. We also look at the opportunities for upward mobility in post-1975 America by examining available research evidence on rates of intergenerational mobility in pre- and post-1975 America. These studies provide evidence of the chances for a son or daughter born into a middle- or low-income working-class family to achieve upward mobility by moving into a higher occupational or income class. Second, we look at America's educational system—primary, secondary, and higher education—because it is the main pathway for upward mobility for young Americans. The availability of equal opportunity through the educational system is the promise of the American Dream, and our task is to assess that promise in America today.

Instead of focusing on the experiences of one group of workers, it will add to our understanding of what is happening in America to compare three different age cohorts and how the Dream has affected them. The first group, which we will call Gen-1, were post-WWII babies born around 1950, and they entered the workforce around 1970 and remained working through the 1980s and 1990s. Gen-1 individuals experienced good times in their early working years, but they would also know firsthand the impact of plant closings and all the other antiworker events of the later decades. These individuals were probably hit hardest by a declining standard of living coming from job loss and lost wages and benefits.

The second group, Gen-2, are the children of Gen-1, and they were born around 1965. They would have grown up with parents who had secure jobs, and by the time Gen-2 were graduating from high school in 1983 there would be awareness among the general public that the economy was changing and that secure jobs and high wages were no longer the norm. Gen-2 individuals would enter the workforce with few expectations about long-term job security, steady wage growth, pensions, and health insurance. They would be the generation that was told over and over by parents and their teachers that they had to work hard and work smart, and the payoff would be lifetime employability with many different employers, but not necessarily lifetime employment with a single employer. You could no longer count on lifetime job security just because you had a job with a major corporation.

Gen-3 are the children of the 1965 cohort, and they were probably born in the 1985–1990 period. By the time they graduated from high school in 2002 to 2007 they would have been provided with detailed information on the earning differences between high school dropouts, high school graduates, and college graduates. All high school graduates in this generation would know the advantages of a college degree. For children of the privileged class, going to college is a no-brainer; the only question would be how much time and effort to put into getting into an elite school. For children of the working class, the question would be "Can I afford college, and if so, where?"

INTRAGENERATIONAL MOBILITY

Intragenerational mobility is a measure of a person's achievements within his/her lifetime and during his/her working career. People may change occupations during their career and they may experience movement into higher-level positions with better working conditions, more rewarding work, and more opportunities for improvement. As one accumulates work experience, it may be accompanied with wage and salary increases, bonuses, and better pension plans.

In the pre-1975 economy, Gen-1 workers experienced wage and benefit increases as they accumulated years of work experience. Labor-management wage agreements often adjusted wages upward to keep up with inflation, and sometimes an increase in addition to the rise in inflation. This has not been the case in the post-1975 economy. The average wages for production and nonsupervisory workers actually declined between 1975 and 2005 when adjusted for inflation; they averaged $17.13 an hour in 1973 and $16.11 an hour in 2005.[2] If this wage rate is received over fifty-two weeks, the 1973 worker had an annual income of $35,630, and the 2005 worker received $33,509, resulting in a $2,121 decline in income.

The effect of flat or declining wages for workers over a thirty-year work career produces a serious reduction in a family's standard of living. Consider the following hypothetical budget proposed by the U.S. Department of Labor for a family of four in 2006. Housing costs $946, food $659, auto $663, health care $196, utilities $293, and five other categories of monthly expenditure add up to a budget of $3,453, or an annual income of $41,436, or a job that pays about $20 per hour. This hypothetical budget is obviously well above the average hourly wage in 2005 and indicates a severe decline in a worker's standard of living as measured by either the hourly wage or the inability to match the Department of Labor budget for a family of four.

While declining wages erode a worker's standard of living on a day-to-day basis, declining pension benefits are a threat to long-term economic security. The preferred pension plan for most workers is a defined benefit plan, whereby the employer makes contributions to a worker's retirement account and from which a worker receives a pension payout based on the total value of the contributions and the accumulated earnings from investments over the course of a work career. In contrast, a defined contribution plan (like a 401(k)) is based on employee contributions over the career, and in some cases employers will make full or partial matching contributions. A worker's monthly contributions to a defined-contribution plan have the advantage of being pretax contributions; nonetheless, they reduce the amount of disposable income that a worker has for monthly living expenses.

In 1980, 84 percent of private sector workers (in firms with one hundred or more employees) were covered by defined benefit plans; this declined to 50 percent in 1997 and declined again to 21 percent in 2005. In contrast, by 2005, some 56 percent of workers had access to defined contribution plans, but only 43 percent took advantage of the opportunity.[3] These data indicate an erosion of the quality of pension plans to workers since 1980.

The above findings on declining wages and changing pensions make it clear that most Gen-1 workers experienced nothing but downward *intra*generational mobility; that is, downward mobility over the course of their careers. Although many of the millions of workers who lost jobs because of plant closings and downsizing found new jobs, only 62 percent worked in full-time jobs, and three-quarters of these workers reported earning less than what they had earned previously.[4]

INTERGENERATIONAL MOBILITY

In many public discussions of social mobility in America, it is often asserted that there is more mobility in America than in Europe, stemming from the European history of having ruling aristocracies and the U.S. tradition of equality following the American Revolution. This may have been true at one time,[5] but recent research evidence indicates that it is not the case today. The *Economist* magazine (May 27, 2006) reported the results of two studies comparing the United States, Britain, European, and Nordic countries on the relationship between fathers' earnings and earnings of sons. Contrary to the belief in the greater openness of U.S. society, a son's earnings more closely resembled those of the father in the United States than in any other country. An added finding is that in the Nordic countries, three-quarters of the sons born in the poorest fifth of the population had moved out of that category by the time they were in their forties, but only one-half of the American men born on the bottom had moved up in income.

These findings on lower rates of intergenerational mobility for Americans versus Europeans may be a surprise to America's privileged class, who like to believe in American individualism, and that people get ahead because of merit. The findings are probably no surprise to America's Gen-2 workers who know firsthand about declining opportunities for mobility. There have been two studies of intergenerational occupational mobility between parents and their adult children. Both studies compared the occupations held by parents and children in the middle and late 1970s and in 1998 and 2004. These studies permitted not only a comparison of the occupations held by parents and their adult children at two points in time but also a comparison when parent and adult children were about the same age.[6] Both studies indicate that there had been more room at the top in earlier years, and less room at the top in recent years. In the 1970s fathers in the highest prestige occupations had far fewer of their children in the same high occupations than did fathers in more recent years. Specifically, in 1973, less than 30 percent of the top occupations were occupied by men whose fathers held the same occupational rank when they were the same age some twenty years earlier. In contrast, in 2004 the sons of fathers who held top-ranked occupations held 51.4 percent of the top positions, and daughters of fathers in top-ranked positions held 43.9 percent of the top positions.

The results of these studies should be approached with some caution, as it is difficult to be confident about comparisons done at two points in time that used different methods. However, the results of the studies of intergenerational income mobility and occupational mobility are very consistent with the general hypothesis that the U.S. class structure has become less open to upward mobility of persons from lower income and occupational groups. One possible reason for the greater hardening of the class structure is that the number of families in the upper privileged class has expanded considerably in recent decades. This means that the sons and daughters of the privileged class were more likely to obtain the level of education needed to fill most of the highest-level occupations. In addition, in recent years more women have entered the labor force in general and have entered high-level positions in business, medicine, law, and academe. Large-scale recruitment of young women and men from lower ranks is necessary only when the privileged class does not produce enough children to perpetuate their class.

EDUCATION AND OPPORTUNITY

Gen-3 Americans (those born in 1985–1990) are currently located somewhere in the educational system, at the primary level, in high school, or making choices about college. Expanding one's years of education and improving performance in the educational system are the two central means by which young men and women can improve their chances to compete for good jobs after completing their education. It is therefore essential that there be equality of educational opportunity for Americans to get the best education that the country can provide. This is not an issue for the sons and daughters of the privileged class, for they already live in communities with resource-rich public schools or are enrolled in private schools that prepare them for entry into the country's very best colleges. But it is an issue for the 80 percent born into families of middle- and low-income working-class Americans.

Money and Opportunity

There is abundant evidence that in today's America the educational system at all levels—primary, secondary, and higher education—is highly stratified and unequal by both class and race. It is unequal by class in three ways. First, the quality of education that is provided students depends on the quality of teachers in schools, the quality of the facilities such as libraries and laboratories, and the quality of enrichment experiences that will enable students to be better prepared for college. Each of these measures of quality in education requires money, and funding for schools is closely related to the income levels and tax base of the community in which the school is located. Second, the parents of children in low-income areas are often dual earners, thereby limiting the amount of time they may have to participate in school activities and the time they have to help students at home. Third, parents with limited income will not be able to provide their children with opportunities for summer camps, for trips to libraries and museums, or for participation in a variety of social and cultural activities that encourage young people to value education. Consider the following description of "how I spent my summer" by two fourth-grade students from families in which parents are in professional occupations.

Top 10 Things I Did This Summer: (1) I went to Italy; (2) I read a lot; (3) I went bike riding and did much better at it; (4) I had play dates; (5) There was a book club meeting at my house; (6) I got a new piano teacher, and my piano playing really got better; (7) I went online more often and improved my typing; (8) I made candy dots and gingerbread cookies; (9) I was involved in a C.U. [California University] research project; (10) I got my school supplies early, and I am looking forward to getting back to school.

The second student reports:

> We had sleep-away camp for two weeks—that was so great. Then Vacation Bible School for a week. Then I think we had a free week. This week they had Boy Scout Camp and swimming lessons—next week just swimming lessons. Then, after that, grandparents come, they have Science Adventure Camp for a week. Then we all go to Hawaii for two weeks.[7]

The researchers report that none of the working class or poor children in the study had summer experiences that could compare with the above reports. This obviously is a case where families with the resources of money and time are able to provide enriched experiences for their children. These stark differences in what families can do for their children must be considered when evaluating the reality of the American Dream and the belief in equality of opportunity. In an earlier book we described the advantages of middle-class children as "hot house kids who had been cultivated for years in an environment of controlled feeding and sunlight." Compared to working-class kids, "They did not yearn for the freedom of adult status, for their sense of self was fused with the wishes held for them by their parent cultivators."[8]

Recent research on childrearing practices in middle-class and working-class families points to the importance of enriching experiences in academic and personal development. Lareau's study of family life contrasts middle-class parents' practices of "concerted cultivation" with working-class practices of "natural growth." The former emphasizes adult-organized leisure activities and extensive involvement with adults as relative equals, while the latter emphasizes child-organized leisure activities and boundaries between adults and children. Lareau believes that these two parenting styles produce middle-class children with a "robust sense of entitlement" and working-class children who "appear to gain an emerging sense of distance, distrust, and constraint in their institutional experiences."[9]

The harsher realities of class inequality in primary and secondary education are based on how schools are funded. Precollege public education is funded primarily from local property taxes and some state and federal funds. The amount of money available to schools for teachers, facilities, and special programs is based on the money raised from taxes on the assessed values of homes and businesses. Communities with more expensive homes and with a stronger business sector will generate more revenue to be distributed to local schools. Per-pupil expenditures by schools is a good indicator of the quality of its teachers (more experienced), class sizes, facilities, and programs. In 2006 the national average of per-pupil expenditures was $13,446. This average obscures very large differences between states and between school districts within states. For example, Connecticut spent $12,323 per student, and Montana spent $8,581.[10] Six districts in New York in 2000 spent $15,084 in the suburbs, and $7,299 in the central city.[11] Everywhere, the pattern is the same: the wealthier the community the more money for better teachers, better facilities, small classes, and enriching programs.

The advantages enjoyed by wealthier school districts extend beyond the tax-base differences that affect per-pupil spending. Although the data are anecdotal, the *Los Angeles Times* reports that at Corona del Mar High School in Newport Beach, California (a predominantly white community), a variety of school-booster groups raise substantial funds for school programs: The PTA raised $50,000 for the high school from a tour of luxury homes; the Super Booster Club raises $35,000 annually to buy supplies for teachers; the Touchdown Club raises $150,000 annually for the school sports programs. In contrast, across the bay at Costa Mesa High School (which has a large percentage of minority students), total funds raised by parents were about $6,000.[12]

Race and Opportunity

Schools are also unequal by race in that predominately white or black schools are a form of *de facto* segregation that contributes to the growing gap in the quality of schools serving mainly whites (in suburbs) in contrast to those serving large proportions of blacks and Hispanics. African American and Latino students disproportionately live in the poorest, mostly urban school districts. In all of the school districts in which three-fourths of the students are poor, at least three-fourths of the students are African Americans. Many of the rest are Hispanics. At the state level, the greater the proportion of a state's population that lives in urban areas, the less that state spends on public education per child, and that is after statistically controlling for the state's wealth and age structure.[13] Integrated schools are more likely to provide better educational experiences in both the academic and social spheres and are less likely to develop stereotyped views of the aspirations and achievements of their students. There is research evidence that blacks and Hispanics who attend integrated schools learn more and perform better in college and in employment.[14]

In heterogeneous schools, whether by class or race, where the children of the privileged and nonprivileged, white and nonwhite, are in the same school, there is a single allocation of funds to that school. In order for that school to be responsive to the needs of students from privileged backgrounds, it will provide better teachers and programs that will also be available to the nonprivileged and nonwhite students. Schools that are heterogeneous are sometimes very clever about how they direct more of their resources to the college-bound students (often from the privileged class). They do so by developing a system of "tracking" that separates students by ability groups and college intentions, which often becomes a substitute for class and race groupings. It separates those students believed to be headed for the labor market from those who are believed to be college bound.[15]

Schools that are in racially segregated low-income neighborhoods operate in a social context that presents major problems for their students. When students in racially segregated schools appear to show little interest in what the school offers to them, it is often assumed to be a reflection of the student's different values, attitudes, limited abilities, and aspirations. The blame is more likely to be placed on the students, and sometimes on the quality of the school programs or teaching staff. The high dropout rate of young black and Hispanic teenagers is often taken as evidence of their failure rather than the absence of a realistic link between school performance and job opportunities. Low-income inner-city neighborhoods suffered major job losses in the 1980s in the manufacturing sector and among workers classified as skilled trade and operators.[16] Young people living in these neighborhoods have fewer job opportunities and fewer adult models of successful working families and are less likely to see school performance as a pathway to a job.

An added problem of living in such neighborhoods stems from the high concentration of poor and unemployed neighbors that can provide support for non-normative, undesirable behavior.[17] Thus, dropping out of high school can be a response to the absence of conventional jobs and the attraction of allegedly more lucrative illegal activities. In addition, unemployment reduces the chances for conventional family life and contributes to early sexual experiences and unmarried pregnant teens and absentee fathers. Some may interpret these behaviors by young men and women as an indicator of their inability to "defer gratification" and therefore an unwillingness to engage in planning, saving, safe or no sex, and studying. But this focus on individual deficiencies fails to account for the structural conditions facing low-income neighborhoods, namely limited job opportunities.

Being a black or Hispanic teenager from a low-income environment (family and community) is a complicated matter. Researchers have found that such students often maintain a belief in two contradictory ideas, which includes a belief in hard work and education as the "way up and out" at the same time that they recognize the reality of their poor housing, the number of jobless adults in the community, and their poor schools.[18] They have a foot in two worlds, and on some days they may believe they do have a chance, and on other days things look very bleak. Thus, some of their deviant or dysfunctional behavior may be episodic and transitory, rather than a fixed and unchanging commitment to a lifestyle that will keep them out of the mainstream of American society.

It is also worth reflecting on the so-called "pathological" and "nonrational" behavior of young black men and women. We referred to it above with the phrase "inability to defer gratification," in sex, violence, drugs, and other forms of immediate gratification. Although these forms of instant gratification are criticized when discussing young black men and women, there is a failure to recognize that many of these same behaviors are often glorified in the media and tabloids when they are exhibited by movie stars, rock stars, and all sorts of cultural and sports celebrities. It is mainstream media that glorifies sexual excess outside of marriage; it is celebrity culture that treats pregnancy outside of marriage as normal and even desirable; it is popular culture that makes drugs an acceptable form of exploratory behavior. Moreover, the above features of immediate gratification are marketed and promoted by corporate movie/media moguls in Hollywood and New York as part of their search for profits from films and music products. While we may not blame the media for the choices made by young men and women in low-income communities, we can surely see how their limited opportunities for stable jobs and future opportunities may predispose them to pursuits that provide short-term and immediate rewards. Moreover, we can surely recognize the possibility that patterns of behavior that are presented in popular culture as normative or acceptable could influence young and impressionable teenagers. In fact, this possibility is supported by recent research by a team of investigators from RAND who surveyed 2,000 adolescents aged twelve to seventeen in 2001 and asked about their television viewing habits and sexual behavior. They were surveyed again in 2002 and 2004 and questioned about TV viewing and sexual activities. Researchers focused on twenty-three programs popular among teenagers that had high levels of sexual content. The researchers summarize their findings by stating: "Our findings suggest that television may play a significant role in the high rates of teenage pregnancy in the United States."[19]

Young men and women from more prosperous and secure backgrounds may also engage in all of the forms of immediate gratification without paying the ultimate price of a totally ruined life. They can recover from all sorts of youthful indiscretions because they have the resources, or more likely their families have the resources, to get them back on the right track. They may spend a year or two "finding themselves" or "sowing wild oats" and then return home and resume a more acceptable educational or professional career.

Popular culture can be a double-edged sword for young men and women who focus on the achievements of celebrity figures. On the one hand, celebrities may provide positive examples of how one gets started on a career in the world of sports or music or entertainment. But popular culture can also be a siren song for many young men and women, leading them to accept unconventional behavior that looks so cool when it is glorified by celebrity culture but may become a trap from which they may never escape. Popular culture should be recognized for what it is; namely, a commercial, profit-driven culture that offers little in return. The movie star, rapper, or sports star should not be the only role models for American youth, but the sad truth is that many low-income communities have few successful adult role models in conventional jobs and few opportunities for young people to enter those jobs.

The cumulative effect of living in a race- and income-segregated school system and being exposed to a destructive popular culture contributes to a loss of hope in the future, which in turn erodes any belief in the value of education as a means of improvement. Whatever might be the mechanisms of cumulative disadvantage, the results are quite clear. A study of the graduation rates from public high schools in 1998 estimated those rates by dividing the number of high school diplomas awarded in 1998 by the number of students enrolled in public schools in the eighth grade in 1993.[20] The researcher found that the national public high school graduation rate for 1998 was 71 percent. The rate for whites was 78 percent, for African Americans 56 percent, and for Latinos 54 percent. Although the study was not able to compare graduation rates for resource-rich schools and resource-poor schools, it was able to report rates for large, urban, inner-city districts. Among the fifty largest high school districts in the United States, Cleveland had the lowest graduation rate of 28 percent, followed by Memphis, Milwaukee, and Columbus.

There are noteworthy differences in the graduation rates across states, suggesting that some schools have found ways to keep students in school and to graduate them. For example, the highest graduation rate for African Americans (71 percent) was in West Virginia, and the lowest rate was Wisconsin at 28 percent. The highest rate for Latinos was 82 percent in Montana, and the lowest rate of 32 percent was in Georgia. For white students, the state with the highest graduation rate was Iowa (95 percent) and the lowest was Georgia at 61 percent. It is hard to know what part of the reason for these different rates is due to the students and what part is due to the schools. We need to learn more about the reason for these big differences among the states in the graduation rates of each racial group of students and devise ways for schools to improve how they can retain and graduate their students.

HIGHER EDUCATION: A TWO-TIERED SYSTEM

The most important long-term trends regarding higher education in the United States are the expansion in the number of persons enrolling and the expansion in the number of institutions offering degrees. In 1900, about 29,000 Americans received college degrees at the baccalaureate level and higher; in 1960 this number increased to 485,600 degrees, and to 1.7 million in 2000. This expansion, especially after World War II, was probably related to major changes in technology that upgraded the skill requirements of many jobs. Higher education became the main way to improve skill levels and prepare people for the higher-skill-level jobs. Some scholars have argued that the increase in educational levels required for jobs has less to do with real skill requirements than being a way that groups holding these desirable jobs protect access from others who also want them.[21] When more people started enrolling in elementary schools, the high school diploma became the requirement for jobs formerly held by people with an eighth grade education. As enrollments in high school increased, the bachelor's degree became the requirement for jobs formerly held by people with a high school diploma. And with the expansion of higher education, with 1.7 million graduates a year, the new credential has become *where* you get your bachelor's degree.

In 2003, a total 16.4 million students were enrolled in 4,070 institutions of higher education, including 2,243 four-year colleges and 1,727 two-year institutions.[22] In an era of small college enrollments, the college degree by itself was a significant mark of achievement and a path to a good job. But when 15 million young people are in college, the market value of a degree is diminished, and people want to know if your degree is from Princeton or Podunk. This new focus on *where* you went to school has introduced a new level of inequality in higher education.

Higher education has become part of the two-tiered system of education that prevents real equality of opportunity and realization of the American Dream. We described above how primary and secondary schools are segregated by class and race. We now see the same thing happening in higher education. In 2000, some 2.8 million students graduated from high school and were eligible to enroll in one of the 2,300 four-year colleges or one of the 1,727 community colleges. In all likelihood, many low-income students and those with weak academic records enrolled in community colleges. Low tuition costs and the ability to live at home while attending school make this an attractive option. What about those who choose to go to a four-year college or university? Among the 2,000-plus schools are about fifty elite colleges and universities where the costs are high and the competition for admission is great. This is where the sons and daughters of the privileged class enroll. A very small number of working-class students "escape" their nonprivileged paths and are admitted to elite schools. Many elite schools have a policy of admitting some "working-class" students and "students of color" who have exceptional academic records and scores on achievement exams. A number of reports indicate that elite colleges have increased their financial aid packages to aid more students from low-income families.[23] The cost of attending schools like Columbia, Chicago, Brown, or Cornell is about $45,000 for tuition and room and board, and a financial aid package for students from low-income families tends to be about $25,000. Elite public universities like the University of California, Berkley; University of Michigan; University of North Carolina; or University of Virginia have lower tuitions (in-state about $10,000 to $20,000; out-of-state about $30,000) and their need-based financial aid packages tend to cover about one-half of the costs. The efforts of many schools to provide financial assistance to low-income students are important, but the number of students receiving need-based aid is small. For example, Harvard has a total of 6,600 undergraduates of which a handful come from families with incomes below $40,000 a year whose expenses are covered by Harvard. But they also have 763 students (11 percent of the total student body) whose family incomes are between $120,000 and $180,000, and Harvard wants to help these "middle class" families by limiting their college expenses to 10 percent of their total family household income per year. Thus, these "middle class" families would only pay $12,000 or $18,000 per year, rather than the regular annual cost of tuition and room and board, which is $45,600 per year.

The elite schools obviously want to become more open to the sons and daughters of all Americans of talent, but their efforts are limited, and they must deal with the fact that they cater to the privileged class and the sons and daughters of that class. It is almost a bad joke to call families earning $120,000 to $180,000 "middle class" when they are simply on the bottom rung of the privileged class. Educational opportunity for talented working-class students will continue to be limited by costs, as the rate of tuition increases at public and private colleges continues to outpace the growth of family income or financial aid packages and is probably greater at public universities than at elite schools.[24]

In addition to the fifty or so elite schools, there are about 200 large state universities with large undergraduate enrollments and large graduate programs that produce many of the doctors, lawyers, scientists, engineers, economists, and managers who become members of the privileged class, although not necessarily near the top of that class. Talented young men and women from the working class are able to enroll in these universities because the costs are well below those of the elite schools. The cost of attending a good state university may be about $20,000 a year (about $7,000 for tuition and the rest for room and board), which is still far beyond the means of many working-class families. For their sons and daughters the challenge is greater, and they often take part-time jobs and take out loans that they hope to repay after school.

When it became apparent in the mid-1970s that the economy was changing and that higher education was becoming more important for entry into the best jobs, the privileged class got the message loud and clear. In 1975, about 40 percent of the children of the privileged class earned college degrees, compared with only about 6 percent of high school graduates from the poorest one-quarter of the population. By 1994, eight of ten sons and daughters from the richest one-quarter of the population earned a college degree, while the attendance rates for the poorest one-quarter increased to 8 percent.[25] Today, almost all the sons and daughters of the privileged class go to college, as do many children from better-paid working-class families. But they do not all go to the same quality schools, do not major in the same fields, and do not enjoy the same rewards after college.

THE MYTH OF MERITOCRACY

As the size of the privileged class has grown, and the levels of their income and wealth have reached previously unseen levels, there is a natural tendency among that class to be a little nervous about their enormous material benefits, especially while everyone else is standing still or sliding back economically. In order to convince the nonprivileged 80 percent of Americans that the privileged deserve their high incomes and wealth, they stress the fact that their achievements are based on talent and hard work. They claim the talent is innate, and the hard work was the years of study and schooling that provided the foundation for their success.

The reality is that most of what they call innate talent and hard work was provided to them through the use of family wealth, which was used to buy high-quality education and enriching cultural experiences for their sons and daughters. After graduating from college, they have available to them a wide range of business and social contacts that set them on a path to high levels of income and wealth. Those who are born into privilege can hardly claim that the benefits of that privilege are evidence of merit.

Most members of the privileged class are there because they were born there, and they inherited their privilege from their parents who provided the means by which they joined their class circle. One study of the 400 richest Americans reported in *Forbes* magazine states that only three in ten of those on the Forbes list can be called self-starters, i.e., their parents did not have great wealth or own a business with more than a few employees.[26] Half of those on this list of wealthiest Americans started their careers with at least $50 million inherited from their family. This is not to deny that there are some in America who started near or at the bottom and may have gone to college and used their knowledge to found successful new businesses. Some like Bill Gates do not even have a college degree, although he didn't start life dirt poor. The self-starters are to be applauded, but they are not evidence that the American Dream is still real and is available to any American who wants to try.

Living in a society with 20 percent of Americans who are privileged by their income, wealth, and job security and with 80 percent working hard to make ends meet while fearing the future puts a very heavy burden on working Americans, *especially if there is a myth of meritocracy.* It is difficult to live in a society with a high degree of income inequality, especially when there is little hope for a better life for you or your family. Every day you are reminded of how good life is for some Americans and how difficult and limiting it can be for others. But people go to work every day because they need to pay the rent or mortgage, to put food on the table, to take kids to Little League games, to be involved in their child's school, and to carry out a whole host of daily routines of living.

We think that it is easier to face your "private troubles" when you live in a society with a low level of inequality than in one like ours that has a high degree of income inequality. We think that this is especially true when people have little hope for improving their lives, and doubly true when they are fearful about their future security. The bottom 80 percent of Americans are constantly reminded of the enormity of the income gap between themselves and their employers, their congressional representatives, their doctors, movie stars, sports figures, and the millions of others whose lifestyles are splashed across TV screens, magazines, and newspapers on a daily basis. Sometimes, in a society caught in the myth of meritocracy, relative deprivation can be more punishing and destructive to the human spirit than absolute deprivation.

A FINAL NOTE ON HOPE

In chapter 2 we provided evidence from 1975 to the present of lost jobs and declining wages for millions of Americans. Many have experienced an erosion of their standard of living to a point where we can say they experienced downward mobility. In this chapter we examined America's educational system to determine if it still provides the means for those who are willing to work hard and take advantage of opportunities to improve their lives. We did not find much evidence of expanding opportunities for working-class Americans to use education for upward mobility. The evidence and arguments presented in these two chapters are the basis for our claim that there is a severe deficiency of hope today for most Americans.

4

Confidence in Institutions

Efforts to assess American citizens' confidence in their institutions has a long tradition, with national polls taken almost every year by several major polling organizations, such as Harris and Gallup. The interest in citizen confidence is based on a belief that the essence of democratic societies is in the commitment of their elected leaders to seek the consent of those governed before embarking on new policies, especially controversial policies. The peoples' confidence in their leaders and institutions is believed to be the basis of legitimacy in democratic societies. It is important to note the distinction between leaders and institutions, because leaders come and go, but institutions are more stable and are based on rules that are expected to prevail no matter who holds the positions of leadership.

Consider the cases of our two most recent presidents, William J. Clinton and George W. Bush. President Clinton had the misfortune of being a married man involved in an embarrassing situation with a young female staff member. It is the kind of thing that happens with some frequency and is sometimes referred to as a peccadillo and treated as a personal matter between the compromised party and his or her spouse. In the Clinton case, however, the matter led to a political crisis leading to impeachment proceedings. Clinton chose initially to follow a path of denial rather than apologizing and seeking forgiveness and chose to go on national television to deny the basic accusation ("I did not have a sexual relationship with that woman . . ."). Subsequent events revealed that the television performance was based on a bold-faced lie that Clinton believed would be successful. When the general public finally recognized his lie, the result was probably a loss of confidence in him as a person, because of his apparent willingness to do anything to maintain his power. But it is unlikely that people lost confidence in the institution of the presidency.

Contrast this with the case of George W. Bush and his decision to invade Iraq to remove its leader Saddam Hussein. The president's decision was said to be based on existing intelligence that Iraq was embarked on a program to develop nuclear capabilities. It is now widely believed among the general public that, at the very least, the president and his top advisers made selective use of intelligence to justify a "preemptive invasion" they wanted for ideological reasons, not security reasons. Those with a less-charitable view of the actions of the Bush administration are inclined to say that they lied, and they did it many times on television (just like Bill Clinton). Many believe that Bush's "lie" severely damaged the presidency, because it called into question the operation of the office or the institution—that a person or group of people could move the machinery of government in a direction not supported by evidence. It should also be stated that many Americans believe that the dispute over the Iraq War is really a political dispute between a president of one party and a Congress of another party.

In this chapter we take a different view about the basis for Americans' confidence in their basic institutions. We do not think that confidence of the sort that provides legitimacy in a democratic society is shaken by lapses in personal conduct, such as Clinton, or even in the questionable decisions of the Bush administration in going to war. Partisans wanted to impeach Clinton, and partisans wanted to impeach Bush; in both cases the partisan fighting was so extensive that the public is more likely to see it as unfortunate wrangling but not threatening to undermine the institution of government. Our view is that the public's confidence in their basic institutions is shaken when the policies of government across administrations from both political parties produce outcomes that appear to be unfair, in that they favor one segment of society over another. Thus, we believe that confidence in America's institutions must be viewed in the broad context of events occurring over the last thirty years—events that were discussed at length in chapters 2 and 3.

HAVE AMERICANS LOST CONFIDENCE?

In 1984, when we were studying plant closings, we talked with workers who had just lost their jobs because their plant had closed and moved to a lower-wage area outside the United States. We asked the workers about the effect that the closing had on their feelings about the government, politicians, and big corporations. While their level of confidence in these institutions was not extremely high, neither was it extremely low, contrary to our expectations. We had expected that the recent shock of job loss would lead them to have little confidence in government and other leaders, but in fact their level of confidence was about that expressed by the general population. Indeed, displaced workers' confidence in the media was slightly higher than that of the general population, and their confidence in labor unions was much higher than the view of the general population. Equally surprising were their answers to two questions: one about whether corporate executives should have a limit placed on how much they can earn, and a second on raising taxes on the rich in order to redistribute income. Contrary to our expectations, displaced workers who were continuously unemployed after the plant closing were no more likely to support these "radical" policies than were other employed workers.

We believe that the reason for these surprising responses from displaced workers was because what was happening to American workers in terms of plant closings and job loss was a relatively recent occurrence and people did not know that they were just seeing the tip of the iceberg that would continue to bring job losses in the future. Moreover, the reality of income and wealth inequality between the top 20 percent of Americans and the rest of society had not yet been widely studied and reported. The first major book on plant closings, *The Deindustrialization of America*, written by Barry Bluestone and Bennett Harrison, was published in 1982. And although there already was a body of research and scholarly writing on inequality, the facts of the magnitude of income and wealth inequality did not start appearing until the 1990s.

Today, when Americans are asked about their confidence in major institutions such as government, corporations, media, or Congress, their responses reveal very low levels of confidence. Table 4.1 shows the results of a Gallup Poll of adults nationwide, conducted on June 11–14, 2007, regarding the percent of Americans who said they had "a great deal of confidence" or "quite a lot of confidence" in the selected institutions.[1]

The only institutions in which a majority of Americans said they had a great deal or quite a lot of confidence were the military (69 percent), small business (59 percent), and the police (54 percent). How can we account for this dramatic difference between what displaced workers said in 1984 and what a majority of Americans are saying today? Our speculation is that the

Table 4.1. Public Confidence in Selected Institutions, 2007

Congress	14%
Big business	18%
The presidency	25%
Television news	23%
Newspapers	22%
Organized labor	19%

American people have finally "gotten it" and are aware of the accumulation of disastrous effects flowing from the failed policies of free trade promulgated by all levels of government in the last thirty years. "Big business" has done what it always does—try to compete in the national and global economy, maximize profits for its shareholders, cut costs, and expand its market share. That is its job in a capitalist economy, and to do otherwise could have serious negative consequences for the company and its leaders. It is the job of government and elected officials to restrain the "appetite" of corporations and protect the interests of the public, which means American workers and American jobs. But what did government do instead?

1. It created tax policies that encouraged corporations to ship jobs overseas and to expand their investments offshore. This has resulted in a trade deficit of over $800 billion dollars in 2007, but that deficit is not just from foreign competition. Almost half of the nation's imports that make up the trade deficit come from the subsidiaries of American companies, or the jobs that could have been done by American workers if the companies had remained in the United States.[2]
2. In addition to providing incentives for companies to ship jobs abroad, Congress continued to support a tax code with a corporate tax rate of 35 percent and enough deductions and tax credits for corporations that resulted in six of ten U.S. corporations and seven in ten foreign corporations paying no taxes from 1996 through 2000.[3]
3. It created trade policies such as the North American Free Trade Agreement (discussed in chapter 2) that resulted in massive loss of American jobs as U.S. companies built facilities in Mexico. To be fair to President Clinton and the Congress that gave us NAFTA, they knew that some workers would be hurt by this effort to help U.S. companies compete in the global economy. So they put provisions in the NAFTA that would assist workers displaced by import competition, such as extended unemployment benefits and money to retrain displaced workers for new and better jobs. Many members of Congress honestly believed that these changes would benefit workers in the long run by preparing them for better jobs in the new "high-tech" economy. But by 2008, even high-level public officials recognized that U.S. trade policies were not working as planned. For example, when Governor Jennifer M. Granholm of Michigan was trying to persuade one of the state's biggest manufacturers to stay in Michigan, promising to build a new plant and providing a new package of tax incentives, she reported the following: "They said, 'there is nothing you can do to compensate for the fact that we are able to pay $1.57 an hour in Mexico.' That's when I started to say Nafta and Cafta have given us the shafta."[4]

Several presidents, such as Bush 41, Clinton, and Bush 43, and the several Congresses that supported them, believed that they were ultimately creating changes in trade policy that would benefit most Americans. They must have listened to President Reagan in 1985, when he included in his report to Congress the following: "The progression of an economy such as America's from the agricultural to manufacturing to services is a natural change. The move from an industrial society toward a postindustrial service economy has been one of the greatest changes to affect the developed world since the Industrial Revolution."[5] One has to wonder what Reagan's advisers were telling him about the marvelous "postindustrial service economy." It could not have been about the loss of a $25-per-hour job and the pressure to take a $10- to $15-per-hour job, if a displaced worker could find one.

There is a lot of talk these days about how Americans have lost trust in their government because "they lied to us about Iraq." That may be so, but that "lie" was understandable to many Americans, given the national trauma of 9/11 and the desire of any leader to avoid being caught flat-footed once again in the face of an international threat. No, the real lie that no one talks about is that our leaders lied to us about the benefits of free trade—maybe not initially, because they thought the United States was facing new global competition—but certainly after each phase of job loss and trade deficits revealed their errors and their failure to readjust their policies. They simply continued to compound their errors and deal with their guilty knowledge of policy failure by a variety of "safety net" measures to soften the blow of free trade. But it was working-class Americans who had to pay the cost of the new global economy, and they are the people who have now passed judgment on their political institutions and are saying very clearly: NO CONFIDENCE to big business, Congress, and the presidency because these are the three main actors who have given the American people the di-saster of so-called free trade. In fairness to the proponents of free trade, the alternative is protectionism, which has its own problems, such as reducing U.S. exports and facing higher costs for imported goods.

If this list of failures of big business, Congress, and the presidency that created the crisis of confidence is not enough, consider the 2008 meltdown of the financial system. The president and Congress developed a massive in-fusion of credit into financial markets in order to provide support for home mortgages that have declined in value and for banks faced with a shortage of cash. This "bailout" of banks and Wall Street firms (those opposing the plan use this term) or "buyout" of mortgages for later resale (those sup-porting the plan use this term) is said to be necessary to restore confidence among U.S. and foreign owners of mortgage-based securities that their loans will be paid. Everyone agrees that this is a crisis that could spin out of control and threaten a slowdown in investment and credit that can result in a long-term recession or even a depression. How is it possible that all the wizards on Wall Street, the federal agencies responsible for regulation, and the congressional committees providing oversight failed to anticipate this financial meltdown?

The Financial Meltdown

There is no easy answer to this question, and all parties share the blame, and we discussed what we believe to be some of the causes in chapter 1 (The New Economy and the 2008 Wall Street Crisis). By way of summary: The first reason for the meltdown was contained in the massive shift in income and wealth that was associated with the transfer of manufacturing jobs and companies from the United States to foreign countries. The average American worker lost jobs, income, pensions, health insurance, and long-term job security. The big winners in the new global economy were Americans with the right educational credentials and in the right industries, like corporate executives, managers, engineers, scientists, doctors, corporate lawyers, accountants, computer programmers, financial consultants, health care professionals, and media/entertainment executives. Their incomes grew in direct relation to the declining incomes of American workers and the declining power of unions to protect workers' jobs and income.

The second major reason for the meltdown was the expansion of the financial sector of the economy that accompanied globalization of production. As the United States stopped being the manufacturer and exporter of products like refrigerators, washing machines, TVs, clothing, and automobiles, the financial sector became the center of all things related to money—investments, corporate mergers, and new ways of making money on Wall Street, like commodity markets, derivative trading, hedge funds, and private equity firms that took over companies for the sole purpose of reselling them. The average earnings of the top twenty-five hedge-fund managers in 2007 were reported to be $892 million, up from $532 million in 2006.[6] The third reason for the meltdown is found in the actions of several presidents and Congresses to facilitate the new forms of investment, and their inaction in failing to provide oversight.

It should be obvious why Wall Street and Congress support the "buy-out" or "bailout" and why the American people are opposed to using their money to support those who have benefitted the most from the decades-long transfer of income and wealth. Most Americans seem to be saying that those who benefitted the most from the wealth bubble should pay the costs when the bubble bursts.

Loss of Confidence in Organized Labor

The next institution receiving low marks from the American people is organized labor. Why is that? The reason is that the leadership of organized labor worked with President Clinton and Congress to pass NAFTA, and this policy was not in the best interests of rank-and-file union workers. Big labor is often in bed with the Democratic Party on important labor issues, and they are often more likely to work with that party than to support a worker-based political party, like the Labor Party. Mark Dudzic, Labor Party national organizer, has been very critical of the Democratic Party because it is dominated by corporate interests, and he has expressed his views as follows: "Democrats . . . are chained to corporate interests that control the money and media that define American politics."[7] They probably also receive criticism because of their failure to protect American workers and their jobs against the efforts of corporations and Congress to weaken labor. Big labor is part of the "old Washington politics," where people believe that they must have a "seat at the table of power" in order to protect their interests, and the way to get that seat is to support winning political parties and candidates. Organized labor chose this pathway to influence rather than to try to mobilize workers to oppose current policies. This view serves to minimize the power of a mass movement of workers, and it underestimates the power of the rank and file if they are mobilized. It is also possible that some national labor leaders are cautious about mobilizing mass-based union power because, once unleashed, that power could become a tool for real reform of the labor movement.

No Confidence in the Media

Finally, how do Americans view the media? How can we account for the low regard that Americans have for newspapers and TV news? We think that one of the big reasons for the negative opinions of newspapers is because of their failure to inform the American people about the big economic changes that were transforming the lives of most Americans. It took the *New York Times* until 1996 to publish a special report on the "Downsizing of America," and only then because downsizing was affecting white-collar workers and middle managers. However, the *Times* never published such a high-profile feature on the millions of Americans' factory jobs that were shipped overseas by multinational corporations in search of greater profits.

On the matter of growing income and wealth inequality, the *New York Times* waited until 2005 to publish "Class Matters," a collection of a series of news articles by their staff about income inequality and declining opportunities for upward mobility. The first article in the series provides a good account of income inequality in the United States and also tells readers about the existence of an enduring pattern of inequality that persists over time. But subsequent articles are more anecdotal and tell a story of Americans at all income levels and how they deal with issues of health care, cross-class marriages (as if that is a major problem for the country), and how people at different levels of income and education usually form social relationships among people very much like themselves. Overall, the articles give the feeling that all Americans face issues of class inequality and deal with it in different ways.

It is the same approach that the *Times* used when it published the "Downsizing of America" in 1996. This account of massive job loss due to free trade and American corporate investment abroad was twenty years too late, and it focused only on the job loss of white-collar workers. Although the *Times* was distressed about the job losses of educated white-collar workers, journalists also wrote of the "guilt of the firing squad," or the terrible responsibility of the top managers who delivered the pink slips. We believe this approach to critical journalism is a fraud because it panders to the notion that we are in this together and calls upon Americans to understand that we are all facing hard times. But the truth of the matter is that we are not "all in the same boat" when facing the challenge of the global economy; privileged-class Americans are riding in a yacht while the other 80 percent are in a rowboat that has a very bad leak.

The other problem with the *Times* series on class in America is that it slips into partisan politics and gives the impression that the Bush tax cuts are what created the high level of income inequality. While it is true that the tax cuts contributed to income inequality, it would have been more accurate to point out that income and wealth inequality is the product of decades of policies on jobs, taxes, education, and health care that have been biased toward the privileged class. Moreover, these policies have been enacted when Democrats and Republicans have been in control of the White House and Congress. The persistent structure of income and wealth inequality is a product of the way the privileged class uses its economic and political power to enlist elected officials to advance its interests.

Another big reason why the American public has so little confidence in television news and newspapers is probably because they have grasped the idea that the so-called media is actually a small number of giant corporations that control most of what Americans read in newspapers and what they see on television. In the United States today there are a small number of large, interconnected media firms with extensive operations in both electronic and print media. They are General Electric, Time Warner, Disney, News Corporation, and CBS Corporation, and they own or control cable television networks, newspapers, radio stations, magazines, and film studios. The products delivered to the public in the form of news and entertainment consistently favor probusiness content and a point of view that does not benefit the working class or a more informed public.[8] The so-called liberal bias of the mainstream media has been the focus of the relatively new conservative pundits like radio talk show host Rush Limbaugh and Fox News's Bill O'Reilly. Although Limbaugh and O'Reilly do not present a progressive or pro-working-class perspective on economic and political news, they have been effective in challenging the mainstream media's one-dimensional view of the world. One result of the new challenge coming from conservative radio talk shows is an increased skepticism of what appears on TV news and national papers such as the *New York Times* and *Washington Post*. Over one-half of Americans get their news from television, followed by newspapers (about 25 percent) and radio (10 percent), which means that the five major media conglomerates noted above are the main source for what most Americans know about national and world events.[9]

It is worth reflecting on the three institutions that receive high confidence from average Americans—the military, the police, and small business. Why are they selected to be regarded with high confidence? After all, there can be a lot of animosity toward police, especially when there are highly publicized events suggesting that police may engage in the use of excessive and unnecessary force or that they may not be respectful of the rights of all citizens. And the military also comes in for criticism whenever the media focuses attention how they are using force in Afghanistan or Iraq. But if there are negative reactions to police and the military, it appears to be in response to specific situations or events, rather than a fundamental distrust of the institution. We think that what these three institutions have in common that commands the support of Americans is that what they do on a day-to-day basis involves considerable risk for the people who get involved; physical risk for military and the police and economic risk for small business owners. In addition, the rewards for what they do are modest. When what you do for a living involves high risk and modest rewards, people are more likely to believe that what you do can benefit others and is not just about self-interest.

A New Spirit of Populism

We think that the declining confidence of Americans in their major political and corporate institutions also reveals a renewed spirit of populism, a spirit that has been encouraged in recent years by national figures like Ralph Nader, Pat Buchanan in the 1996 election, and John Edwards's speeches about the "two Americas" in the 2004 election. Nader has consistently attacked both political parties for being influenced by corporate donations to their political campaigns and for ignoring the real concerns of the American people. When Buchanan ran against Bob Dole to be the Republican nominee in the 1996 presidential election, he attacked NAFTA, immigration policy, and corporate greed, and often provided the following kind of rhetoric: "When AT&T lops off 40,000 jobs, the executioner that does it, he's a big hero on the cover of one of those magazines, and AT&T

stock soars," and "Mr. Dole put the interest of the big banks—Citibank, Chase Manhattan, Goldman Sachs—ahead of the American people."[10]

The populist spirit rests on criticism of the wealthy and powerful corporate executives, bankers, bureaucrats, and politicians for their excesses at the expense of the average American. Populism attempts to rally discontented Americans eager for change, and it does so with reference to the *haves* versus *have-nots*, the *fat cats* versus the *common man*. Ralph Nader's lifetime of battles with corporate giants on behalf of the American consumer served as the basis for his entry into presidential politics in 2000 and 2004 under the banner of economic populism. Pat Buchanan's run for the presidency in 1996 was also based on an appeal to working-class Americans with rhetoric like: "The voiceless men and women in this country have no one to represent them in Washington because the hierarchy of both parties really argues on behalf of those trade deals [NAFTA], which are often done for the benefit of corporations who shut their factories and move them overseas."[11] When John Edwards was the vice-presidential nominee of the Democrats in 2004, he railed against the "two Americas," "one for people who live the American Dream and don't have to worry, and another for most Americans who work hard and still struggle to make ends meet."[12] When he ran to be the presidential nominee of the Democratic Party in 2008, he focused his attention on poverty in America. He stopped talking about the "two Americas" because he got "beaten up" by the mainstream media for his "class warfare."

This renewed populist spirit has contributed to a call for reforms that recognize the importance of the needs of the average American in the economic, political, and social arenas. The direction that will be taken by this new populism is uncertain, for it can take two different paths. It can become focused on economic inequality and become the basis for a mass movement calling for greater redistribution of wealth in the form of policies directed toward better social security benefits, higher wages, job security, and single-payer national health care. The money for these new programs would come from increases in corporate income taxes, higher income tax rates on the rich, and a new tax on wealth. This new wealth tax would relieve the guilt felt by a Warren Buffet who says that his maid pays a higher tax than he does because all her money comes from taxable income while his money may come from tax-free bonds and other investments protected by the tax code. Populist reforms would also push for serious reductions in defense spending and the reallocation of funds to rebuild decaying cities, transportation infrastructure, and inner-city schools. This would be a progressive expression of populism, consistent with some of the messages of Ralph Nader and John Edwards.

But the new populism could also turn in a direction of a reactionary populism of the sort found in the messages of a Pat Buchanan. Anger over the results of thirty years of free trade and globalization could produce a new protectionism in trade policies and a renewed isolationism directed against immigrants. It could also see greater withdrawal into new identity politics based on the narrow interests of religion or ethnicity. Jean Hardisty's analysis of resurgent right-wing conservatism illustrates how reactionary populists used Americans' insecurity stemming from economic restructuring to mobilize resentment against government and hostility to a wide range of liberal policies.[13] This form of populism can only be offset by a kind of class-based politics that puts broad economic interests first, because they have the potential to benefit people of all religions, races, colors, or ethnicities.

ELITE INTERESTS AND CONFIDENCE IN INSTITUTIONS

Up to this point we have argued that Americans' low level of confidence in their political and economic institutions can be traced to their experiences over the last thirty years with job loss and declining wages and opportunity. This would certainly be the case for working Americans who make up 80 percent of the population. But what about the other 20 percent, those more privileged because of their secure high-paying jobs or their educational credentials? Do the more privileged Americans also lack confidence in their political, economic, and media institutions?

We ask this question with tongue in cheek, because national polls on Americans' confidence in their institutions rarely report results for the upper-income classes, and also because it would be silly to believe that the privileged class lacks confidence in the three big institutions that consistently deliver policies and information that are to their liking. It is likely that wealthy and powerful Americans think of themselves as having a major say in how the dominant institutions are operating. If they are unhappy with tax policies or trade policies, they can turn to their business lobbies like the U.S. Chamber of Commerce or the National Association of Manufacturers to contact members of Congress with their concerns. If doctors are unhappy with current or proposed policies on Medicare or Medicaid payments, they can turn to the American Medical Association to represent their concerns. Wealthy and powerful Americans, through their contributions to both political parties and members of Congress, have purchased *access* to the sources of political power, which they use to protect their interests. Elite Americans do not think about confidence in their institutions but about their effectiveness in getting Congress, agencies of government, and the president to do their bidding.

Consider the following example of how the privileged class acts when they have doubts about the direction of U.S. trade policy in the new global economy. In February 1998, the *New York Times* published a two-page open letter to the Congress of the United States entitled "A Time for American Leadership on Key Global Issues."[14] The letter was written at the time when Congress was considering legislation that would extend NAFTA-like agreements with other countries in Latin America, and such legislation would be of great benefit to American corporations and banks to extend their investment activities in new settings. Such legislation would be harmful to the job security of working Americans, just as the earlier NAFTA agreements contributed to massive loss of manufacturing jobs and large trade imbalances.

The letter was signed by 132 persons who are undoubtedly privileged-class Americans, including two former presidents (Carter and Ford), forty-two former high-level public officials (Secretaries of Defense, Treasury, CIA, etc.), and eighty-eight presidents of major corporations. Why would these 132 elites take the time and spend the money (about $100,000 for printing an ad) to engage in this "American-as-apple-pie" form of political expression? Surely, this group of elites had already expressed their concerns to individual senators, representatives, federal agencies, and even the president. Were they trying to reach "Joe Six-Pack," or the average American who does not read the *Times*? Not likely. What they were doing was mobilizing the millions of other members of the privileged class across the nation to use their influence (political contributions, phone calls to congressional representatives, letters to the editor) to push this issue. They were trying to reach doctors, lawyers, journalists, scientists, managers, stockbrokers, media executives, think tanks, and opinion-shaping groups, and to enlist their support.

As we stated above, privileged-class Americans seek to shape and influence their political, economic, and media institutions, rather than to express their degree of confidence in those institutions. When elite Americans do express a lack of confidence in a particular institution it is usually based on a set of *interests* that are of importance to them. The interests of small business owners might be primarily economic, and they would monitor tax policies that affect their business; if things don't go as they wish they might express low confidence in Congress. Similarly, the interests of scientists might focus on federal funding for research on cancer or AIDS, or stem cell projects, and they would be unhappy if the federal budget did not reflect these interests. Let us illustrate how elite interests may be reflected in their confidence in institutions.

Elite Americans are those with educational credentials and high incomes, and they are likely to be more involved in national and local organizations reflecting political interests, cultural interests, health interests, and educational interests. They also are more likely to participate in single-issue activist organizations that reflect their concerns about abortion, teaching evolution in schools, stem cell research, global warming, poverty, or affirmative action. It is our view that elite-class Americans reveal their confidence in institutions according to whether they believe that their interests are being advanced or thwarted by the actions of persons associated with relevant institutions.

In order to test this idea, we examine the results of a small-scale study conducted in a single small city.[15] The study focused on people's views of science, and it selected sixty people who were members of single-issue groups that could be affected by the work of science and scientists. There were five groups in the study, and ten persons were selected from each group. They included *feminists* (ten PhD holders involved in a Women's Studies program); *environmentalists* (ten members of local chapters of national environmental organizations such as Audubon and Sierra Club); *religious fundamentalists* (ten pastors of fundamentalist churches); *political left* (ten leaders or very active members of national political organizations guided by liberal or socialist principles); and *political right* (ten leaders or very active members of local politically conservative organizations). All participants were college graduates, and a majority had advanced degrees and would therefore qualify as part of an educational elite.

The ten persons selected from each group were interviewed about their views of science and, luckily for our purposes here, they were also asked about their confidence in institutions other than science. They were asked whether they had "a lot," "some," or "hardly any confidence" in thirteen institutions and professional groups. Those who reported "a lot" of confidence in this local study would be comparable to those members of the general adult population from the national poll data reported above, who said they had a "great deal" or "quite a lot" of confidence in specific institutions.

The findings from this study confirm our view that elite Americans try to protect their "turf" when they express either great confidence or no confidence in institutions; they like the institutions that they believe support their interests and criticize institutions that they believe harm their interests. Members of the different interest groups expressed very different views of institutions. For example, only 12 percent of feminists and 12 percent of members of political left groups expressed "a lot" of confidence in the medical profession, but 71 percent of religious fundamentalists, 55 percent of the political right, and 44 percent of environmentalists said they had "a lot" of confidence in the medical profession. We believe that the reason for these large differences is that the feminists and political left respondents believe that the actions of the medical profession do not advance their groups' interests on issues like reproductive rights for women or support for socialized medicine policies. Another example is their confidence in labor unions; only members of the political left groups (50 percent) expressed "a lot" of confidence in labor unions, but only one person from the other four interest groups expressed any confidence in labor unions.

The five interest groups—feminists, environmentalists, fundamentalists, political left, and political right—were in agreement with the national poll data (presented above) from the general population for three institutions: Congress, journalists, and major corporations. Not a single person from the five interest groups expressed confidence in these three institutions. These findings are interesting because the three institutions deal with a broad variety of issues that can affect the interests of many groups. Congress considers legislation and discusses policies that affect feminists (reproductive rights), environmentalists (energy policy), fundamentalists (stem cell research), and political left/right (market-centered programs or government programs).

In summary, we believe that the low level of confidence expressed by working-class Americans in Congress, media, and corporations is a reaction to decades of collusion between political leaders and corporate leaders to enact policies that advance corporate interests at the expense of the jobs, wages, and benefits of working Americans. In contrast, members of privileged groups are not experiencing the same job insecurity and limited resources as workers, and thus express their confidence in terms of their group interests as religious leaders, feminists, or environmentalists. Working-class Americans face threats to their families and their economic security, which we may call "survival interests." In contrast, elite Americans face threats to their values (e.g., right to life, air pollution, stem cell research), which we consider to be secondary to questions of survival.

WHOEVER PAYS THE PIPER CALLS THE TUNE

Many of the national polls that have assessed Americans' confidence in their state institutions and corporations have also asked questions about basic principles of democracy; namely, that it is government of, by, and for the people. A CBS News/New York Times poll conducted on May 10–13, 2000, asked adults nationwide: "How much say do you think people like yourself have about what the government does—a good deal, some, or not much?"[16] Sixty-four percent said "not much," 25 percent said "some." Only 10 percent said a "good deal." The same joint poll was conducted on July 11–15, 2004, and a nationwide adult sample was asked: "Would you say the government is pretty much run by a few big interests looking out for themselves or that it is run for the benefit of all the people?" Sixty-four percent said "a few big interests," and 28 percent said "all the people."

These poll numbers suggest the existence of a considerable gap between the people and the government; a level of disconnect or alienation that does not fit the "of, by, and for the people" ideal. We think that one source of this alienation is the expanded role of money in politics. After the Democratic and Republican primaries selected their nominees for president in the

November 2008 election, the two candidates embarked on campaigns that spent over 1 billion dollars to get their message before the voters. Television and print media present daily updates on what various candidates are saying or doing, and we also get daily or weekly accounts of the fund-raising efforts of candidates, and estimates of a candidate's strength are often discussed in terms of their success in attracting campaign contributions. Contrary to the media's view of money in campaigns, there may be a hidden message about money that is being communicated to the average American. Maybe the medium (money) is the message.

The role of money in politics ("money is the mother's milk of politics") has been a corrupting force. The most obvious corruption is the oft-reported quid pro quo arrangements between politicians and big contributors that often lead to convictions and prison terms for the contributors and the politicians. There are many high-profile cases of alleged and proven corruption that cannot have escaped the attention of average Americans. The most recent case is that of Jack Abramoff, a lobbyist who pled guilty to three criminal felony charges involving theft of over $20 million from clients while presumably working with members of Congress on behalf of his clients. The Abramoff case also led to the conviction of two White House officials, one member of Congress, and nine other lobbyists and congressional aides.

More frequent cases may not involve illegality, but impropriety, or the appearance of corruption. A good example is the 1989 case of five senators who were accused of improperly aiding the chairman of a failed savings and loan bank that was under investigation by a federal oversight agency. The senators were alleged to have approached the chairman of the federal investigating agency with a request that he "ease off" the investigation. The senators' defense was that what they did was not illegal and that they were following normal congressional practices to aid a constituent. That defense is weakened by the fact that the five senators had collectively received $1.3 million in campaign contributions from the chairman of the failed bank, which cost American taxpayers $3.4 billion in bailout costs.

Perhaps the most flagrant example of the "it's-legal-but-appears-to-be-corrupt-defense" is the practice of earmarks, which involves members of Congress adding pet projects for their constituents or home communities to legislation developed for other purposes. Earmarks are inserted into legislation without identifying the member of Congress who sponsored the earmark, and they direct funds to specific projects or recipients without a public hearing or review. In 2004, there were 14,211 earmarks inserted into legislation with a total cost of $52.69 billion. Earmarks may be directed to schools, universities, community projects, or private companies. There has been a $325,000 earmark for a swimming pool, $200,000 for a rock and roll museum, $200,000 for a deer avoidance system, and $3 million for dust control. Citizens for Responsibility and Ethics in Washington (CREW) provides an interesting analysis of this practice. One report issued by CREW identifies what they believe are the twenty-two most corrupt members of Congress who have used their positions for financial benefit of themselves, their family members, or their friends.[17]

It is worth noting that Democrats were very critical of the Republican-controlled Congress for their involvement in pork-barrel projects through the use of earmarks in legislation. Still, when the Democrats regained control of Congress, the number and dollar amount of earmarks increased. A health and human services appropriation bill for 2009 contained $618 million in earmarks compared to $278 million in 2008. The total number of earmarks requested in bills for fiscal year 2009 was 3,796, worth about $2.7 billion.[18]

The biggest role of money in politics involves the millions of dollars that must be raised by candidates running for Congress and the presidency. The Center for Responsive Politics reports that in 1996 the money required to cover all aspects of an election campaign was $367 million for a presidential campaign, $7.3 million for the Senate, and $1.14 million for a House seat. In the 2008 presidential campaign, Barack Obama raised over $600 million and John McCain raised over $300 million. Both candidates liked to say that the majority of their donors contributed less than $200, but they didn't say that the majority of the money comes from wealthy individuals, corporate political action committees, and business and professional groups. Those who give the big money expect something in return, and what they get does not necessarily benefit most Americans who are sitting on the sidelines.

ACTIVISM, INTERNET, AND INFOTAINMENT

During the last fifty years there were two periods in which Americans' confidence in their institutions reached such low levels that it helped to spark two national social movements against the federal government's international policies. These two antiwar movements involved millions of Americans who had become so disenchanted with their institutions that they went into the streets to express their discontent and thereby produced a major crisis of legitimacy. The first was the anti–Vietnam War movement of the 1960s, which was precipitated by the U.S. government's decision to send troops to Vietnam to support the South Vietnamese government, which was fighting the North Vietnamese and Viet Cong. It was a conflict that the United States decided to enter after the French withdrew following their defeat in the battle of Dien Bien Phu. Involvement started slowly, when President Kennedy sent in advisers to assist the South Vietnamese military. This small-scale decision would soon spiral upward and draw two other presidents, Johnson and Nixon, into an escalation that would reach 500,000 troops and over 50,000 American deaths on the battlefield.

Americans came to see the battle between the North and South Vietnamese as a civil war that was of no interest to this country. The U.S. government across three presidential administrations chose to see the war in the frame of the Cold War struggle between the United States and the Soviet Union, and the conflict between the two Vietnams as part of a domino theory that required U.S. involvement to stop the Communists from spreading their influence throughout Southeast Asia. Opposition to the war among Americans was expressed through mass mobilizations in the streets of Washington, D.C., in dozens of cities, and on hundreds of college campuses. Many demonstrations were peaceful, and many were violent. Demonstrators were often beaten, jailed, and even killed. Civil disobedience reached critical levels and the legitimacy of America's political institutions was the first to be discredited, but the crisis would soon spread to challenge broader social institutions of the family, education, and the criminal justice system.

The second antiwar movement emerged in the 1980s and came to be known as the Central America solidarity movement. In this period, the U.S. government decided once again to intervene in the affairs of other countries, in this case the Central American nations of Nicaragua and El Salvador. The United States was unhappy with the Sandinista government in Nicaragua because of their Socialist and Communist inclinations. The Sandinista Front for National Liberation (FSLN) had toppled the Somoza regime, which was pro–United States but very unpopular among average Nicaraguans. The United States did not intervene directly with troops, but it did everything it could to topple the Sandinista regime, including creating and supporting a military force in Nicaragua (the Contras) that they hoped would topple the Sandinistas.

Another Central American country, El Salvador, also presented a problem for U.S. policy in the region that was committed to supporting regimes friendly to the United States. The government of El Salvador was led by José Napoleón Duarte, and it was engaged in a political and military struggle with indigenous opposition from the Farabundo Martí Front for National Liberation (FMLN) and its political ally, the Democratic Revolutionary Front (FDR). The United States channeled substantial military and economic aid to the Duarte government in the hope of defeating the insurgents.

Opposition to U.S. policy in Central America was expressed through public demonstrations, petitions to Congress to cut off aid to the Contras in Nicaragua and the Duarte government in El Salvador, and support for organizations that provided aid to the Sandinistas and to the opposition groups in El Salvador. One of the most notable groups was the Committee in Solidarity with the People of El Salvador (CISPES), and they had chapters in many communities across the United States and central headquarters in Washington, D.C.

In both historical periods, the 1960s and the 1980s, there were mass mobilizations of people to attend public rallies, to raise money to support activists who had been arrested, to sign petitions, and to engage in a variety of collective acts of civil disobedience. All this took place during a time when there were no wireless phones, no iPods, no BlackBerries, no personal computers, no Internet, no blogs, no MTV, no Facebook, no YouTube, and no dozens of other pieces of personal technology that Americans use today to communicate with each other and to access information. How was it possible that without modern technology such as the widespread use of personal computers and the Internet that so many people were mobilized to engage in mass demonstrations that were successful in opposing government policies in Vietnam in the 1960s and in Central America in the 1980s? The answer is the pencil-and-paper telephone tree, used by hundreds of activists to use landline telephones to call preassigned recipients and inform them about a planned demonstration, film, speaker, petition, or fund-raising project. It was a combination of dedicated people and a specific plan of communication, along with announcements in local newspapers about such events. Newspapers were willing participants in the dissemination network as long as you provided written announcements, media packets, and the promise of a potential clash of opinions. Media survive on conflict.

There are two counterexamples of contemporary social activism that has been facilitated by Internet-based mobilization. In 1999, tens of thousands of activists came to Seattle, Washington, to protest against the World Trade Organization and its free-trade policies. Designed to be a peaceful protest, it developed into a full-scale confrontation with Seattle police and the National Guard, who used pepper spray and tear gas to prevent the protesters from disrupting the WTO conference. The assemblage of protesters representing labor, environmentalists, and human rights groups was undoubtedly facilitated by communication across Internet networks.

A second case of Internet-facilitated social activism was the United States Social Forum in June–July 2007 in Atlanta, Georgia. Between 5,000 and 10,000 trade unionists, peace activists, and community organizers assembled in the name of global justice and anticapitalism. For five days, they attended workshops, plenary sessions, cultural events, and street actions.

The question of old style (telephone trees) and new style technology (computer and Internet) as ways to reach people brings us to the question of activism in the age of the Internet. The advent of the personal computer and the Internet led many to believe that we were on the brink of an age in which there would be a new democratization of media,[19] because the Internet would make it possible for citizens to limit the power of traditional media (newspapers and television) to control what is presented to the public. The symbol of this new age of the Internet became the MySpace/MTV "presidential dialogues," and the CNN/YouTube presidential debates that used questions submitted by YouTube users.[20] These efforts were especially attractive to young voters because of their extensive use of social network-ing Internet sites and because of young voters' limited interest in reading newspapers.[21] The Internet has also facilitated the mobilization of millions of Americans for political campaigning and fund raising, and web-based media have enabled people to work around elite-based media that are in-creasingly distrusted by groups across the political spectrum.

We think that the jury is still out on the significance of personal comput-ers and the Internet for an empowered citizen participation in politics and for the development of greater confidence in political institutions. It is our belief that after an initial burst of enthusiasm for the Internet as a tool for enhanced political participation and a bottom-up framing of issues and mobilization of people, there will be the same level of disenchantment with the medium that had already been expressed toward traditional me-dia. Why do we believe this to be so?

First, Internet-based activism is a very efficient and cost-effective way to use direct mail lists to get contributions, obtain petition signatures, and direct-letter-writing/e-mailing campaigns directed at political of-ficials. However, it is a very passive form of participatory politics and is less directed at bringing people into the streets than in creating new social networks of "friends" and personal ties. These networks have the potential to become activated, as we observed in the Battle for Seattle, but it has yet to be demonstrated that public mass activism is here to stay as a new form of political expression. Second, the amount of information that flows through the Internet is enormous and is not subjected to any standards of oversight or objectivity. This leads to a dependence on blogs as a way to cut through the overwhelming amount of information presented to Internet users. But bloggers provide little confidence to readers about the objectivity, fact versus rumor and gossip, of the ideas presented in their blogs, to say nothing of the identity and possible false personas of blog-gers. Third, the dependence on blogs for political discourse can encourage a discrediting of facts and objectivity and encourage people to think that politics is all about opinion anyway. Bloggers are competing for audience attention, and this will always encourage sensational claims over reasoned arguments, given the limitations of time and audience attention span. The erosion of reason and argument in political discourse cannot contribute to the creation of new and more legitimate social institutions or to having greater confidence in leaders or existing institutions. In the competition for audience, bad blogs (sensationalism) will always drive out good blogs (reasoned analysis). Politics is always a mix of reason and emotion, but when it becomes all emotion the consequences are deadly. If the choice is between watching a TV documentary on Paris Hilton or Eleanor Roosevelt, we are all in trouble.

The final source of the erosion of Americans' confidence in their institutions can be traced to the increasing tendency in all media, traditional and modern, to blend entertainment and information. The ideal example of this blending is *The Daily Show* on Comedy Central TV, which is devoted to satirical analysis of news. While obviously a comedy show, the use of real news items as the basis for humor generates such audience response that the show seems to provide a model for serious news shows. Consider, for example, the most popular news shows on TV: *The O'Reilly Factor, Hannity & Colmes, Hardball with Chris Matthews,* and *The McLaughlin Group.* Each show has a blend of regular panelists and guests who discuss the issues of the day presented by the host. Each of these shows operates at a high decibel level where participants often speak simultaneously and try to outshout each other to make their points. They frequently have the look of squabbling kids around the family table, with the father-figure host trying to maintain some semblance of order and coherent discourse.

This blend of information and entertainment on these shows apparently works as a way to attract a viewing audience and to keep them coming back. It is hard to doze off while watching these shows, and it is sometimes hard to separate the heat from the light. Contrast this form of infotainment with more staid programs such as *News Hour with Jim Lehrer* on public television, and on commercial television, the late Tim Russert's *Meet the Press* and *This Week with George Stephanopoulos.* The format of these shows is serious extended discussion of a limited number of news topics, and often with a structure of two or more guests or panelists discussing a topic of some importance. The viewer is usually presented with two sharply divergent views on a subject, but in a very orderly manner. The questioning of guests is serious and often seems designed to extract quotable comments that will be picked up on the next day's national news shows.

The problem with the conventional serious news shows is that their content is often of interest mainly to the inside-the-beltway political class, and their guests are usually lawmakers and government officials, and rarely union leaders, workers, or populist interest groups. Research on television news shows indicates that they rarely have guests who will challenge mainstream opinion or represent the interests of average Americans. As one media watchdog group stated: "True advocates for the left—people who actually push for progressive social change and identify with left-of-center activists—are almost invisible on TV."[22] Moreover, people of color—blacks, Latinos, Asians, and Native Americans—are significantly underrepresented in newsrooms and on the national TV broadcast side of the business.[23]

The age of the Internet contains the promise of a new way to bring Americans back into politics and perhaps to restore their confidence in their leaders and institutions. That promise has yet to be fulfilled.

5

Identity, Grievance, and Trust

Should a person vote for Hillary Clinton so that we can have the first woman president? Should a person vote for Barack Obama so that we can have the first black president? Should we vote for or against any candidate based on their gender, race, ethnicity, or religion? Although these questions surfaced in connection with the 2008 presidential election, they have been the basis for numerous social issues and public-policy conflicts facing Americans in the last thirty years under the name of *identity politics*. Identity politics in its broadest meaning is about the attitudes and actions of groups based on their race, ethnicity, gender, or sexual orientation that focus on their differential ability to influence decisions that affect their lives.[1] The term has been used with increasing frequency in U.S. politics since the 1970s.

However, before discussing identity politics it might be useful to say something first about group identity, which must exist before it can be expressed in a political form. The identity of any group is a product of how its members view themselves and how others view them. The self-definitions of a group may be based on a common language or culture, common historical experiences, or current circumstances, and member ties to the group may be extensive or limited. Identity may also be imposed on a group, as in the extreme case of slavery in America. Being part of an identity group can provide one with a sense of a shared bond that provides support in times of need, or under conditions when people move to new cities or new countries and seek others who share their culture.

The importance of identity groups based on race, ethnicity, or gender may have grown as there has been an apparent change in people's patterns of participation in a wide range of voluntary associations. In 1994, Robert Wuthnow reported research evidence indicating that there was a new form of voluntary association, which he called "support groups," that were appearing in America in greater numbers and varieties, and which he described as follows: "a small group that meets regularly and provides support or caring for those who participate in it."[2] In concrete terms, they are singles' groups, youth groups, women's groups, prayer fellowship, or men's groups. Wuthnow believed that the trend reflected a retreat from participation in large-scale, rational, bureaucratic structures and a return to more intimate, community-based, voluntary associations. In 1995, Robert Putnam published an article entitled "Bowling Alone: America's Declining Social Capital," in which he presented evidence indicating a decline in membership for all categories of voluntary associations in the United States.[3] Putnam believed that the small support groups identified by Wuthnow tend to be self-absorbed, inward looking, and therefore lack interest in issues affecting the wider community. We are interested in these questions because we are concerned with whether or not the pattern of participation in voluntary groups contributes to fostering a sense of community and trust among Americans who participate in a wide variety of groups.

We are also interested in whether the changing patterns of voluntary association and small-group membership may be associated with the role played by identity groups in American life. Members of identity groups often have a shared history, culture, or language that provides the kind of primary bond that is missing in traditional voluntary associations that have a more diverse membership in terms of their social backgrounds. In addition, members of an identity group may come to recognize a shared past or present grievance that leads them to consider collective action outside of their group. It could be a grievance that is local, like school programs for their children, or national, like equal pay for equal work. When a group uses its identity in an instrumental fashion to try to influence the actions of others in the larger society in ways that may benefit their group, it enters the realm of identity politics.

There are several aspects of identity politics that should be considered. First, although this form of politics has been associated with grievances based on race and gender, it quickly expanded to include many ethnic groups and many other personal qualities such as sexual orientation and physical disability. Second, the specific grievance that serves as the unifying condition for the group is a particularistic grievance, in that it may be claimed by a subset of Americans and excludes those who do not have the quality or experience that is the basis for grievance. Third, those Americans who are excluded from the aggrieved group are asked to acknowledge the validity of the grievance and to support remedies designed to benefit the aggrieved group. Fourth, if the grievance is about oppression that had its origins in the past, the cost of the remedies is to be paid by persons who may believe that they played no part in the original oppression. Fifth, those who make grievance claims based in the past may not be suffering from the effects of that oppression today. For example, educated, middle-class blacks may identify with the historic oppression of slavery, but their current lives may not limited by that historic oppression. Similarly, Jewish Americans or Italian Americans or Irish Americans may all have valid historic claims of oppression (anti-Semitism, Hollywood stereotypes of Italians, Irish immigrants as unreliable workers), but their current lives may not be shaped by that historic oppression.

An imposed group identity can inhibit the development of public policy to assist disadvantaged groups. For example, in the 1980s, attacks on social welfare programs by conservative groups often connected welfare with race, and welfare recipients were depicted as if they were all African Americans, when in reality there were more whites on welfare.[4] Welfare recipients were also framed as "nondeserving poor" when they were given the image of "welfare queens" who would drive in fancy cars to pick up their welfare check. This race-based attack on welfare recipients served to create divisions between white and nonwhite poor, despite their common interest in having a social safety net. The image of the nondeserving poor surfaced again in the mid-1990s, when both political parties and both houses of Congress voted to "end welfare as we know it," and President Clinton signed the Personal Responsibility and Work Opportunity Act. The 1996 law ended the Aid to Families with Dependent Children (AFDC) and ended the federal guarantee of cash assistance to poor families.

Although welfare mothers come in all shades, colors, and ethnicities, they came to be identified with one race, thereby making it easier for politicians to attack the existing welfare program and to replace it with a less caring and more punitive system.

The grievances of groups involved in identity politics are usually valid. But the five features of identity politics discussed above often serve to divide Americans who have other common interests and deflect attention to the intergroup conflicts between blacks and whites, men and women, Hispanics and blacks, Asians and blacks, gays and straights, and so on. In order to build trust among different interest groups there must be a simultaneous recognition of their separate grievances and what unites them in common grievances.

In contrast to the particularistic grievances often associated with identity politics, there is a universalistic grievance that a majority of Americans are (unfortunately) eligible to experience. That grievance is associated with a family's current income, job security, and educational opportunities. Limited income and opportunity is an equal-opportunity grievance that may affect any American regardless of gender, race, or ethnic group. And more important, it is a grievance that may be used to unify diverse groups of people to push for public policies that could benefit many Americans.

This universalistic grievance is often referred to as *class politics*. At one time Americans were more interested in class politics than in identity politics. What are some of the reasons for this change?

There are several plausible reasons for the increasing interest of Americans in their racial, ethnic, or religious identity, and thereby, the rise of identity politics. We think that one reason is associated with our discussion in chapter 4 concerning the decline in confidence in America's major political and economic institutions. As Americans became less secure about their jobs and their futures, they lost faith in government and corporations, and they looked for support in troubled times to others who were very much like themselves. Uncertain about their future and unable to rely on the government for help, they turn their attention to community groups who could provide aid and comfort in time of need. Joining an identity group provides an opportunity to discuss common concerns and experiences, to obtain information about available resources such as jobs, and a chance to act collectively to deal with shared concerns. We think that growing insecurity and declining trust in government may also be related to the increased interest in religion as an identity group in America. Let us illustrate.

In the social sciences there is the long-established idea that links economic development to secularization. That is, as society becomes more advanced and modern, especially with regard to improved economic, educational, and social conditions, the population comes to rely less on religion as a significant part of their lives. Two scholars have described this idea in the following way.

> We believe that the importance of religiosity persists most strongly among vulnerable populations, especially those living in poorer nations, facing personal survival-threatening risks. We argue that feelings of vulnerability to physical, societal, and personal risks are a key factor driving religiosity, and we demonstrate that the process of secularization—a systematic erosion of religious practices, values, and beliefs—has occurred most clearly among the most prosperous sectors living in affluent and secure post-industrial nations.[5]

There is support for the theory of secularization among most affluent Western European nations, Canada, and Australia, where churchgoing has declined in the last two decades. The exception is the United States, which has high rates of religious participation. However, the researchers do not see the United States as an exception to the secularization idea. They stress the fact that the United States is the most unequal postindustrial nation under comparison, and that its citizens "face serious risks of loss of paid work by the main breadwinner, the dangers of sudden ill health without adequate private medical insurance, vulnerability to becoming a victim of crime, as well as the problems of paying for long-term care of the elderly. Americans face far greater anxieties than citizens of other advanced industrialized societies about whether or not they will be covered by medical insurance, be fired arbitrarily, or be forced to choose between their jobs and devoting themselves to their new-born children."[6] In short, because survival is more uncertain in the United States compared to Western European nations, there is greater importance of religion in the lives of people with a weak social safety net.

A second reason for the increased interest in identity politics is the failure of past class-based movements, most notably the union movement. After a period of major gains in union membership and strength after World War II and continuing into the 1950s and 1960s, there has been a continual decline under the impact of globalized production, labor-displacing technology, and antiunion government policies. In addition, the union movement did not always provide strong leadership in support of the full participation of African Americans and women in their ranks, thereby undercutting the universalistic potential of this class-based movement. We believe that the decline of the union movement, and class politics, left a vacuum that would be filled by a variety of identity groups.

A third reason for the increased interest in identity groups can be traced to the declining belief in a "melting pot" America, where the processes of assimilation and integration would eventually bring everyone together under a common set of values and cultural practices. Although inequality based on race and ethnicity may have declined, it has not disappeared, and it stands as a refutation of the goal of assimilation. We now turn to a discussion of the rise and decline of the goal of assimilation in American life.

THE RISE AND DECLINE OF ASSIMILATION THEORY

In the 1950s and 1960s most Americans shared a belief in how the American Dream worked, and that belief was that the country welcomed people from all over the world to become Americans and that becoming American was achieved through a process of "assimilation and integration." The assimilation-integration idea was born out of the experiences of millions of immigrants who came to the United States in the early part of the twentieth century. They arrived in the United States speaking languages other than English and with knowledge of customs, traditions, and social practices that were part of their home country but had to be modified or discarded in order to live in America. Upon arrival in their new national home these immigrants found themselves at the bottom of the social ladder, but they did not believe that they or their children were destined to remain at the bottom. When immigrants started their new lives in America they usually lived among their coethnics who spoke their language and who could provide advice and support as they found places to live and work. After receiving support from others who preceded them, they would eventually be able to give help to others in the same way that they had been helped. The assimilation story told the new immigrants that their place at the bottom of the social ladder was temporary and that they would gradually become assimilated into their new country. The assimilation process, as described by some sociologists, contained the following steps or stages.[7]

1. The first and most difficult step is acquiring the language of the new country. This is often difficult for the adults because they are living among coethnics and are still speaking the language of their home country. Children from immigrant families who are attending school learn English more quickly and often assist adults in this process.
2. The next step involves acquiring the values, beliefs, and symbols of the dominant culture, which may include clothing, food preparation, and family life.
3. After assimilation based on language and culture, the next barrier is joining the groups and organizations of the dominant society. This involves contact with others in the workplace, friendships across ethnic or racial lines, and joining civic organizations that are not limited to one racial or ethnic group. This type of assimilation is more difficult than cultural assimilation because it involves leaving one's ethnic community and joining a mixed ethnic community.
4. Next is marital assimilation, which is facilitated by contact with men and women from other ethnic and racial groups. A high rate of intermarriage between first- or second-generation immigrants and members of the dominant culture facilitates a weakening of ethnic identity. Identity is now based on participation and success in the mainstream institutions of the society.
5. The final stage involves a change in attitudes and behavior of dominant groups who become more receptive to members of ethnic groups and less likely to harbor prejudicial attitudes and engage in discriminatory practices.

Assimilation theory had its day, but it started to unravel as a realistic idea during the civil rights era. The early stage of the movement for civil rights had an assimilation-integration thrust as black Americans sought an end to the so-called separate but equal society. The movement called for equality in public accommodations, schools, neighborhoods, and an end to Jim Crow institutions. The early message of Dr. Martin Luther King, as a national leader of the civil rights movement, had integration as the goal, where people would be judged by the content of their character and not by the color of their skin.

As the spotlight was placed on the conditions under which black Americans lived during 240 years of slavery and 100 years of Jim Crow segregation, it became apparent that very little had changed with respect to jobs, income, and opportunity. Assimilation theory may have worked for white ethnics as each generation of sons and daughters of Italian or Irish immigrants moved up the educational and occupational ladder, but black Americans seemed to be running in place. Assimilation for African Americans or Native Americans was obviously much slower than for white ethnics, raising the possibility that prejudice and discrimination were deeply embedded in American social institutions and that competition and conflict were the normal conditions of intergroup relations.

The decline of the assimilation narrative was further facilitated by the assassination of Dr. Martin Luther King on April 4, 1968. Many believed that King became a threat to the status quo when he began to link issues of race with issues of poverty and when he raised questions about how the war in Vietnam was responsible for America's lost war on poverty. King's assassination was followed by the assassination of Robert F. Kennedy on June 5, 1968, during his bid for the presidential nomination; his political platform contained a strong populist message about poverty in America.

The assassination of these two national leaders, who were in many ways reformers and believers in the goal of integration, added to the disappointment and disillusionment of many activists for civil rights and equal opportunity. Disappointment with the promise of assimilation was also a product of the growing tendency in political circles to blame the slow progress of African Americans on deficiencies within the disadvantaged group rather than the failure of the institutional structure to adapt to the needs of the disadvantaged group. The most prominent example of this tendency was the so-called "Moynihan report," a Department of Labor report titled *The Negro Family: The Case for National Action*.[8] The authors, Daniel Moynihan, then assistant secretary of labor, with the assistance of Paul Barton and Ellen Broderick, argued that the history of slavery and subordination had such a marked impact on the Negro family that many Negroes would be unable to take advantage of the new opportunities that were made available to them (". . . at the heart of the deterioration of the fabric of Negro society is the deterioration of the Negro family").

The Moynihan report generated substantial controversy in government circles, the civil rights movement, the press, and among academic social scientists.[9] This controversy coincided with the rise of a critique of "melting pot" America referred to as pluralism theory. This idea stressed maintaining patterns of ethnicity because the "maintenance of distinctive cultural, organizational, and behavioral characteristics is often a way of coping with discrimination."[10] As pluralism took hold, many race and ethnic-based opposition movements were asserting the validity of their culture and their rights. Advocates of the cultural Black Is Beautiful theme and the political Black Power theme turned away from the belief in integration and assimilation and emphasized instead self-help community organizing and many forms of black interest-group politics. The women's movement and other ethnic-based political groups soon embraced this model of identity politics. Identity politics following the black movement were often directed at the many forms of discrimination that affected a group's material interests, such as jobs, income, worker rights, and educational opportunities.

In recent years, however, identity politics has increasingly focused on the cultural domain and on what we might call the "micro insults" inflicted on a group when they seek recognition for their "cultural rights." Consider, for example, the following story reported by the Associated Press on March 5, 2008: "For Muslims, Harvard tests women-only gym hours." Harvard University banned men from one of its gyms for a few hours a week to accommodate Muslim women who say it offends their sense of modesty to exercise in front of the opposite sex. As one might expect, there was opposition from some students who thought it unfair to deny access to a facility that is supposed to be for everyone. Supporters of the policy stated that "the majority should be willing to compromise. It's just basic courtesy. We must show tolerance and respect for all others." A more telling defense raised the fairness principle: "We get special requests from religious groups all the time and we try to honor them whenever possible."

This incident may seem amusing because the stakes are so low (how can one offend women's modesty in the age of YouTube and Facebook?), but it has all the ingredients of many of the contemporary issues raised by identity politics. Consider, for example, the annual Christmas event in many communities across the country when religious groups attempt to place a Christmas scene (typically a manger scene) in the town square, in a public park, or around a central courthouse. The requests of the Muslim women or the Christmas-scene advocates can be seen, of course, as very modest and reasonable and consistent with calls for tolerance and respect for all beliefs. The problem is that the requests involve the use of public space and involve inconvenience for some citizens to accommodate the requests of other citizens. It also raises the question of competing experiences of "offense." The Muslim women or the Christmas-scene advocates are offended by circumstances that conflict with their modesty norms or offended by efforts to take Christ out of Christmas. Those who are unsympathetic to these requests assert their own feelings of having their tax dollars used to support activities that offend their beliefs in separation of church and state.

Public officials or university administrators who are faced with these requests may wish to be tolerant and respectful, but they are also worrying about the slippery slope of requests that may follow. What guideline will they use to separate valid requests from frivolous requests, and isn't the judgment of what is valid and frivolous in the eyes of the beholder? There may be only two standards that can be applied to adjudicate requests like those of the Muslim women or the Christmas-scene advocates: would anyone be offended by the activity, or is public space open to all requests regardless of anyone's opinion of validity? If no person or group objects to the religious identity requests, or if any person or group can request use of public space for a display (subject only to scheduling limitations), then let all identity requests be honored.

Another example of micro insults based on cultural differences between identity groups was experienced by one author in a study conducted in a unionized manufacturing plant. During the course of the research a conflict emerged between some white and black workers over the display of symbols that each group found offensive. It started when a complaint was lodged with the human resources department claiming that some workers were displaying the Confederate flag at their work stations, typically on their lunch boxes or tool boxes. The accused workers, who were white, responded that they were also offended by black workers who wore T-shirts with Black Power symbols or Malcolm X quotes. The human relations people wouldn't do anything without support from the union, and the union did not want to take a position that would engender conflict within the union. The resolution was to ban both the flag and the T-shirts, a decision that both groups rejected on the grounds that their culture was being disrespected.

When identity groups fight with each other in their versions of victimhood battles to see who has the biggest grievance, neither side wins very much. Both sides are distracted from larger issues that should unite them, like having better wages, greater job security, pensions, or paid sick days.

This brings us to the sensitive questions of who is in charge of identity groups, and how do they decide on their priority issues? Who in identity politics groups makes the decisions about which issues to take before the public for remedy? Who decides whether their group should focus on stem cell research, abortion, gay marriage, religion in public places, hate crimes, or on income and wealth redistribution? We don't know the answer to this question, but we can make an educated guess. The leadership cluster in many national identity politics groups are typically people with educational credentials and some experience in leadership roles. They probably enjoy somewhat higher social and economic standing than the rank-and-file members of their identity politics group. In fact, they may often be members with privileged backgrounds, as measured by their family income, wealth, and general level of security. This being the case, why would a privileged-class leadership select income and wealth redistribution as the central social issue that requires attention when it would not be in their class-based interests?

One could not raise this question about the interests of leaders and rank and file in the civil rights movement, when the struggle was to achieve equal standing before the law and all persons of color would realize the same benefits. But many contemporary identity groups contain a diverse membership that may differ along class, race, or religious lines, and these differences may shape their goals and strategies. Choices must be made about whether to stress past grievances or current grievances; cultural respect or income inequality. There may be different interests between identity groups, and there may be different interests within identity groups. But before these groups can begin to trust each other and to work together, they must begin to understand their respective grievances. With this objective in mind, we now move to examine the question of past and present grievances of dominant identity groups in the hope that we may identify things that have the potential to divide Americans and things that may unify them.

GRIEVANCES: PAST AND PRESENT

Grievances abound in America. It is likely that almost every American can tell a story of prejudice or discrimination experienced by a member of his/her family. This almost universal experience of grievance is due to the fact that every American family either immigrated to this country voluntarily or was brought here without their consent. Native Americans have the distinction of having already been here when the Europeans arrived, and African Americans were brought here against their will and subjected to legal discrimination under slavery and Jim Crow laws after slavery was abolished. Upon arrival, every immigrant family probably was confronted by groups who were already here and who found something about the new arrivals that offended them. The white ethnics who flocked to America in the late nineteenth and early twentieth century experienced a variety of forms of prejudice and discrimination.

During the large immigration waves of the late nineteenth and early twentieth centuries, new arrivals often lived in ethnic enclaves in large cities. At this time there was an understandable tendency among new immigrants to preserve cultural traditions and to keep their "mother tongue." The strong ethnic identities of the first wave of immigrants often declined as their children attended school, became speakers of English, and absorbed prevailing popular culture. Although some assimilation was occurring and ethnic enclaves declined in size as people migrated out, there was still a pattern of ethnic festivals that attracted first- and second-generation Italians, Germans, or Irish to acknowledge their ethnic heritage. We would call this a "soft" form of ethnic identification, reflected in a desire to acknowledge and maintain cultural practices that were brought to the United

States while still adopting new practices that were dominant in the new setting. This was the intergenerational pattern of assimilation and integration described earlier.

Although all early ethnic groups had difficulty with assimilation and integration, extreme hostility toward them often occurred when they shifted from being an ethnic group to being an interest group, which we might call a shift from a "soft" form of ethnic identification to a "hard" form. Let us illustrate the soft form with a personal example. When the first author was fourteen years old he joined the Italian Sport Club (his uncle already was a member), a bicycle road-racing club composed of first- and second-generation Italian teenagers, young men, and older men. The younger members spoke standard vernacular English, while the older men used many styles of "broken" English, often mixing English and Italian. In the same city there were also French and German bicycle-racing clubs. (Cycle racing was very popular in Italy and other Western European countries, and the tradition was maintained in the United States.) Every Sunday morning during the warm seasons there were intraclub and interclub road and sprint races. All bike riders wore a distinct jersey (the same style as worn by bikers in the Tour de France today), and the Italian club colors were red, white, and green. Although the club colors were those of the Italian flag, that association was unspoken at weekly races, monthly club meetings, or annual awards banquets. The colors were recognition of a common heritage and culture, not a political statement. That is "soft" ethnic identification.

Contrast the above anecdote with the experience during World War I when the term "hyphenated American" became an epithet hurled at some foreigners and was used to disparage Americans who displayed an allegiance to a foreign country. Even more remarkable is that the epithet was used at the time by a former and a current president of the United States. Hyphenated Americans became an issue when some German American and Irish American groups called for U.S. neutrality at the start of World War I. This produced great hostility toward immigrants who were charged with having divided loyalties. Describing this period in a book in 1955, John Higham wrote:

> The two most distinguished men in public life lent their influence to the antihyphenate movement. Theodore Roosevelt bestrode the movement; Woodrow Wilson surrendered to it; and together they illustrated the change that the progressive impulse was undergoing. Roosevelt stood out as the standard bearer and personification of unhyphenated Americanism. Wilson's final address in support of the League of Nations [delivered September 25, 1919, in Pueblo, Colorado] stated: any man who carries a hyphen about with him carries a dagger that he is ready to plunge into the vitals of this Republic when he gets ready.[11]

One might speculate that the antihyphenate movement was stimulated by the political actions of German and Irish Americans to influence foreign policy, and thereby becoming an interest group expressing "hard" ethnic identification. When an ethnic group celebrates its history and culture, it does not require anything of others except for understanding and respect, and the result can be a healthy diversity. And all Americans have a heritage to celebrate if they should choose to do so. But when a group takes a position in an arena of economic, political, or value questions, it can expect a pushback from other groups feeling that their interests are being threatened. We offer this distinction between soft and hard ethnic identification as perhaps one way of understanding the basis for intergroup hostility and lack of understanding.

The common experience of grievance in every American family doesn't mean that all grievances have equal standing in their initial and continuing impact on the targeted group. In the next section we examine the grievance claims of identity groups and distinguish among them on two dimensions. The first dimension is the severity of the harm inflicted in terms of the numbers involved and the extensiveness of the harm. In some cases, the harm could be extensive, such as genocide, but the number or proportion of the group affected is small. The second dimension is the degree to which a past harm continues to affect the targeted group today. Thus, we separate grievances on two criteria: a severity dimension and a past-present dimension. The point of this analysis is to find grounds among identity groups for understanding their grievance claims.

NATIVE AMERICANS

Past: When Europeans arrived on the eastern shores of the New World, there was an indigenous population of between 1 million and 5 million people that we will refer to as Native Americans. There were numerous nations of American Indians who were already living within the borders of what would become the United States, and they were certainly not "discovered." Scholars of Native American demography estimate that between the time of initial European contact (about 1600) and 1850, the Native American population declined from about 2.5 million to 200,000.[12] This extraordinary decline of population was undoubtedly due to a combination of factors including stolen land and starvation of displaced peoples, infectious diseases brought by the Europeans, and outright killing of Native Americans in the so-called Indian Wars.

Present: From the low point of 200,000 Native Americans, there has been a gradual increase, especially after 1950, to a population today of about 4 million. It is believed that this population growth is due to better health

programs that reduced infant mortality and to more Native Americans being willing to be so identified at census time. Most Native Americans live
in the Southwest, and only about one in five live on reservations. Current
social and economic conditions of Native Americans indicate that they do
not compare favorably with other Americans. Educational levels of Native
Americans are far below those of other ethnics and white Americans.[13]
About 71 percent of Native Americans graduate from high school, and
11.5 percent are college graduates, compared to 84.6 percent high school
graduates for white Americans and 27.2 percent college graduates. For black
Americans the figures are 80 percent for high school and 17.3 percent for
college; for Hispanics it is 57 percent high school and 11.4 percent college;
and for Asian Americans it is 87.6 percent high school and 49.8 percent
college graduates.

The income level of Native Americans is about two-thirds that of white
Americans. They are underrepresented in white-collar occupations and
overrepresented in blue-collar jobs, resulting in about 23.2 percent of Native Americans living below the official poverty line in 2000. This is the
highest poverty rate among all ethnic groups.[14]

AFRICAN AMERICANS

Past: The conditions of life under slavery are difficult to imagine. Considering only the legal conditions under which the institution of slavery operated
conveys some idea of what it was like for the first Africans in America.[15]

1. Blacks were to be slaves for life.
2. Slaves were *both* property and persons; owners held title to blacks as
   property and had some responsibilities to blacks as persons.
3. Children would inherit their mother's status as a slave.
4. Christian baptism did not automatically lead to freedom.
5. Marriages between blacks and whites were prohibited.
6. Blacks could not acquire or inherit property.
7. Blacks could not engage in litigation or enter into civil contracts; they
   could not testify against whites in court, nor could they sit on juries.

Although there was concern about "humane treatment" for slaves, there
was little doubt about their "biological inferiority," which extended to the
postslavery period and their continued exclusion from education, jobs,
housing, and civil rights. The legacy of slavery continued for the 90 percent
of blacks who remained in the South after slavery was abolished. They lived
primarily in rural areas and were tied to an agricultural economy that per-
petuated their oppression. World War I brought the first wave of migration

of blacks into northern cities. The decline of external immigration during the war and the need to meet wartime production goals combined to serve as a major impetus for the migration of black Americans. World War II led to a second major wave of black migration from the South to northern cities.

Present: In 2006, there were 36.6 million African Americans in the United States. The cumulative effects of 350 years of oppression under the institution of slavery and Jim Crow laws, to say nothing of the informal levels of prejudice and discrimination, can be measured in numerous years in which unemployment rates were two or three times the national average, and a 2006 poverty rate of 21.6 percent, only slightly below Native Americans.[16] The high school graduation rate of blacks in 2003 has improved to 80 percent (national average is 84.6 percent), but the college graduation rate of 17.3 percent is well below the national average of 27.2 percent.[17] The median income of African Americans is about 60 percent of white earnings. In addition to their low levels of income and wealth, they are saddled with high levels of single-parent households, poor housing, inadequate neighborhood schools, and a general pattern of dependency on public assistance. Many of the present problems of black Americans can be linked to the residential segregation patterns that keep them locked into areas with poor job opportunities, poor housing, deteriorating neighborhoods, and limited public services. In 2000, almost 87 percent of blacks lived in metropolitan areas with high levels of residential segregation.

HISPANIC AMERICANS

Past: In the mid-1800s there was a significant Spanish-speaking population in the southwestern United States. They were there along with Native Americans to welcome the incoming white ethnics from the East. Treaties between Mexico and the United States guaranteed basic citizenship rights to Mexicans living in the new American territories. As the white ethnic population grew, Mexicans were pushed to the margins and their culture and language was overwhelmed. As the Southwest developed, an increasing number of Mexican immigrants came to the United States as a source of cheap labor and experienced the beginnings of prejudice and discrimination between the "old" and "new" Mexicans.

Present: The Hispanic population was 38.8 million in 2000, making them the largest ethnic group in the United States. About 80 percent of Hispanic Americans are Mexican in origin, with another 20 percent Puerto Rican and Cuban Americans. Their poverty rate is 19.3 percent (2006), ranking them a close third behind Native Americans and African Americans.[18] Their rate of graduation from high school is almost one-half that of non-Hispanics (44 percent), and their level of college graduation is well below the national average (11 percent). Mexican Americans' jobs are far below national averages of upper-level white-collar jobs, and they are also below the participation level of Puerto Ricans and Cuban Americans.

ASIAN AMERICANS

Past: Asian Americans are another diverse ethnic group like Hispanics but even more heterogeneous. They are Chinese, Filipino, Japanese, and Korean, and they do not share the same language (in contrast to Hispanics) or culture. According to the 2000 Census there were 13.1 million Asian Americans, with Chinese and Filipinos being the two largest groups. Asian Americans entered the United States voluntarily in search of opportunity. The earliest to arrive in large numbers were Chinese, and they came to the West Coast in the mid-nineteenth century to work in mining and railroad construction. Their experience was similar to other ethnic immigrants, meaning the usual stereotyping, prejudice, and discrimination. They shared the same disadvantage of other ethnic groups of color in that their greater visibility made them a greater target for unequal treatment.

The most significant example of formal/legal discrimination was against Japanese Americans during World War II. In March 1942, President Roosevelt signed an Executive Order requiring 110,000 Japanese Americans to be relocated to internment camps in six western states and Arkansas. The relocation took place rapidly with the cooperation of those being interned. In the process, Japanese Americans were forced to sell homes and businesses at prices far below their true value. They were released from the camps in January 1945. Several government commissions were established to compensate Japanese Americans for their losses, but claims were limited to $2,500. In 1980, a second commission was established to reexamine the question of compensation, and its recommendations included an official apology to the Japanese Americans and a payment of $20,000 to each of 60,000 survivors of the internment camps.[19]

Present: The achievements of Asian Americans in the realms of education and occupational attainment are exceptional. Their educational attainments and occupational positions exceed that of other ethnic groups, even white Americans. Their level of poverty is far below other ethnic groups, and slightly above that of white Americans.[20] Despite their achievements, they continue to experience informal expressions of prejudice and discrimination, and in some cases violence. Current tensions for Asian Americans are related to issues of growing economic competition with Asian nations, especially China. The movement of jobs overseas and the outsourcing of work to Asian countries continue to create a negative climate for Asian Americans.

WHITE ETHNICS

Past: White ethnics are made up of the millions of white immigrants who came to the United States voluntarily at the end of the eighteenth century and the beginning of the nineteenth century. The largest groups were English, Irish, German, Italian, Polish, and Jewish. Although they had different languages and culture, what they had in common was the absence of physical characteristics that made them easily identifiable. We say this despite a literature discussing how Italians or Irish "became white," which argues that a commingling of racial and ethnic stereotypes created forms of discrimination similar to what was experienced by immigrants of color. All of these ethnic groups experienced prejudice and discrimination, but the Irish and Italians were singled out for special hostility, due perhaps to the added hostility toward Catholics.

Jewish Americans came to the United States with an exceptional historic experience of persecution. Their oppression was highlighted during World War II when 50 to 60 million civilians died, including 6 million Jews in the Nazi concentration camps. The extreme persecution of Jews in Nazi Germany and elsewhere precedes their entry into the United States; thus, they are less likely to be seen as long-standing victims of oppression in this country, as is the case with Native Americans and African Americans. Since the Holocaust was a German crime and the criminals were not Americans, the grievance claim of Jewish Americans is different from that of other groups.

Present: White ethnics have entered the mainstream of American society with many exceptional achievements in the social, political, and economic realms. The advantages of white skin and European origins reduced the number of obstacles that white ethnics faced. Although all white ethnics may be exposed to continuing prejudice and stereotypes, especially their depiction in television and Hollywood movies, they are more likely to fall into the realm of micro insults rather than large-scale discrimination and exclusion.

WOMEN

Past: Women are the final identity politics group. Their grievances may be those that are shared with each of the other identity groups that were already here to greet the Europeans. Alternatively, they came voluntarily or as involuntary immigrant groups. Their unique grievance is a history of being treated as second-class citizens, either because of being viewed as lacking intellectual capability or being emotionally and biologically hampered from entering the public roles available to men. Although they always carried out vital domestic household roles that involved both family life and economic roles, they have always been under the oversight and control of men.

As an identity group they lack the specific historically linked grievance of a common land theft, as with Native Americans, or subjugation as property, as with African Americans. What they may lack in terms of the severity of the harm inflicted, they make up for in the scope of their grievance. All women, regardless of color or ethnicity, experienced a similar form of exclusion from public life.

Present: As has been the experience of white ethnics, women have entered almost all areas of mainstream life. Their educational attainments are exceptional, and they have moved into many of the established male professions of law, medicine, and biological sciences, although their gains have been smaller in fields such as engineering, mathematics, and physics. Their grievances today focus on equal pay for equal work and breaking remaining barriers into the highest positions in corporate America, the professions, and academe. Additionally, there still remain many occupations that are gender segregated, such as the predominately female occupations of elementary schoolteachers and nursing and many predominately male blue-collar occupations.

SUMMARY

In summary, it should be clear that of the various identity groups examined, only Native Americans and African Americans may lay claim to both historic and current grievances. This conclusion is based on the two criteria we applied to grievance claims, namely the magnitude of the harm experienced by the target group and the continuity of that harm over time. Hispanic Americans are a close second in terms of the current level of harm experienced, but not on the harm experienced when first incorporated in American society. The white ethnics and women also fall short on both of the grievance criteria.

This review of past and present grievances of identity groups is important because such groups claim grievances as the basis for any specific remedies that they propose. There often are competing claims of experienced grievances among identity groups because grievance claims are the basis for competing for public attention and public resources to remedy their grievance. Since the number of claims usually exceeds the available public space in media for their coverage, the competition for public attention drives identity groups to fashion their grievances in the most dramatic way. It also can lead to "grievance wars" among identity groups. Roger Cohen, in an op-ed article in the *New York Times*, raises the question of why there is a "magnificent Holocaust Memorial Museum" in Washington, D.C., when there is no memorial of equivalent stature "dedicated to the saga of national violence that is slavery and segregation."[21] The answer lies in the relative power of the groups making grievance claims.

Grievance claims are usually fashioned in a manner to gain support from other groups who see a way to advance their agenda while they help some other groups. For example, a prochoice women's group might fashion their grievance claim in a way to attract a group interested in a broader question of women's reproductive health.

Since this chapter is concerned with the question of trust among Americans (rather than trust in institutions as discussed in chapter 4), we believe that grievance wars can have a number of unanticipated consequences. First and most obvious, it may produce tension or conflict among groups that really have more reasons to be united than divided. A good example of this tension between identity groups with competing claims to the "greatest grievance" is the competition for public attention that often occurs between black Americans and Jewish Americans. The second unanticipated consequence is that the growth in the number of grievance claims made by identity groups can lead to saturation and "grievance overload." Too many grievances and too much repetition of the same grievance can lead the general public to "turn off" all the messages from identity groups asking for support.

MAKING UP FOR PAST GRIEVANCES: COMPENSATORY OPPORTUNITY

The 1976 Democratic Party platform contained the following statement: "We pledge vigorous federal programs and policies of *compensatory opportunity* (italics added) to remedy for many Americans the generations of injustice and deprivation." The phrase "compensatory opportunity" would become better known some years later as "affirmative action," a set of policies used primarily in employment and education that redress past discrimination against members of minority groups. Many would say that the original intent of affirmative action was to focus on African Americans, but it was expanded to include sex, religion, national origin, and any other condition or characteristic that became the basis for discrimination. This expansion was accompanied by a change of terminology in academe about its goals regarding the student body. More attention was given to *diversity* when discussing the student body. This shifts attention from the black-white mix in the student body to a mix of women, international students, Asian students, physically disabled students, and so on. This helped universities to look heterogeneous, but it did not help African Americans gain access to college.

The idea of affirmative action is a good one; nevertheless, it is flawed and generates great resistance. The problem is that it makes all members of a group eligible for favored treatment without requiring any evidence that all members share the same disadvantaged current conditions. Thus, all African Americans would be considered to be eligible for preferential treatment in admission to educational institutions even though some of those African Americans enjoy better economic conditions than some members of another group with less favorable economic conditions. Let us make this issue concrete with the following personal example.

Both authors of this book are academics and we have often served on committees responsible for selecting minority applicants for special fellowships. The process of rating applicants typically produces a list of applicants ordered by their academic achievements, special experiences, and personal essays that reveal special qualities. There is usually considerable agreement about the top two or three applicants for fellowships, and it is often the case that although these applicants are deserving of the fellowships, they really do not need them in an economic sense. Highly qualified applicants often come from families with one or two professional parents who also have educational credentials. They have had the advantage of going to resource-rich high schools and being provided with enriching life experiences at home and in the community. The "losers" in the competition often have good academic records, but not as good as the "winners," and they often also come from less advantaged families. Thus, minority applicants for a fellowship who have less economic need are favored over minority applicants for whom the fellowship might make a life-changing difference. There are millions of talented African American women and men who can succeed in college if they had the economic resources to attend.

The advantage that is enjoyed by the economically privileged black applicant for college admission or a fellowship is the same advantage enjoyed by the economically privileged white applicant. The advantage comes from having attended resource-rich high schools that expect their students to attend college and from having enjoyed the cultural capital of activities and experiences that can be purchased with money and that contribute to academic performance. Under the current rules of affirmative action, men would be excluded from the gender-based affirmative action, and whites would be excluded from the color- or ethnic-based program. This would be true even if all the male and white applicants were in life situations of greater current economic disadvantage than any of the qualifying applicants of gender, color, or ethnicity. This is the source of opposition to affirmative action, namely a belief that it is unfair.

Whether or not the above-described situation is very likely to occur, it is what the average person thinks about when she/he expresses opposition to affirmative action. So what can be done to save the idea of affirmative action, while making it fairer and more acceptable to most Americans? Here is what we propose for consideration. Add economic disadvantage to affirmative action programs when admitting and funding people for college from the categories or color, ethnicity, or gender. In order to redress past and current grievances, colleges would admit and fund some of their applicants who are economically disadvantaged, talented, and deserving. Economic disadvantage would be determined by family income and wealth; talent would be determined by a broader range of qualifications besides academic performance in high school and test scores; and being deserving would be determined by the applicant's life activities that reveal a determination to improve one's life and the lives of others and being the first person in the family to attend college. Every American high school student with a current economic disadvantage would be eligible to compete for admission to college and for funding of college tuition and living expenses, although the highest priority would go to African American applicants because of their more valid claim of past and current grievances.

If a new affirmative action program that included economic need were to be established, it would need to be combined with an effort to identify potential college-bound students early in their high school careers, so that they could begin to think of themselves as college material and thereby aim their social and academic life toward this new goal. This effort could be undertaken in each state by a joint program of colleges and universities (especially publicly funded schools) to identify those high schools in their state with a large number of students from economically disadvantaged backgrounds. With funding from the federal government, the institutions of higher education in each state could take responsibility for a cluster of eligible high schools and begin entering those schools to identify first- and second-year high school students who exhibit the talent and motivation necessary for college admission.

There have been other arguments for creating a class-based system of affirmative action. Richard Kahlenberg in 1997 proposed that affirmative action in higher education and employment should be based on economic disadvantage. Similarly, Walter Michaels in 2006 published a book critical of the failure of American society to acknowledge the way "injuries of class" affect lives, and instead is more preoccupied with matters of identity and diversity.[22]

Critics of the call to include class in affirmative action in higher education admissions have argued that it could hurt African Americans because the much larger number of poor whites would "crowd out" applicants of color, or that Asian Americans would be the biggest winners because of their relatively low income and high test scores.[23] However, since African Americans are disproportionately poorer than whites they should enjoy more opportunities from the inclusion of economic considerations for admission and funding.

It is also important to recognize the difference between the goal of diversity in higher education and class- or race-based affirmative action.

Diversity is based on the idea that some groups are underrepresented in college and that their inclusion would enrich the educational experience of all students. This is an admirable idea, but it will not address the goal of affirmative action, which is about compensation for long-standing exclusion and disadvantage. The group with the most valid grievance claim that calls for compensation is economically disadvantaged African Americans.

Any effort to introduce class-based criteria for affirmative action must be careful not to make things more difficult for low-income African Americans. Even very strong supporters of race-based affirmative action who are cautious about changing the policy recognize the merits of a class-based policy. For example, Jane Hardisty has concerns about class-based policies because of the larger number of low-income whites over low-income blacks. However, she also states the following:

> A formula for affirmative action that takes race, class, and gender into account would be complicated to administer and may not be substantially more popular with the voting public than the current race- and gender-based policies. It may open the door to demands for affirmative action considerations from a broad range of groups that suffer discrimination and lack opportunity. Because race is so prominent in the hierarchy of American prejudices, the hostility to affirmative action "preference" may persist in a "reformed" affirmative action that considered class as well as race and gender. But it would improve the fairness of affirmative action and better, if imperfectly, serve the goal of compensatory justice.[24]

We believe that an affirmative action program of the sort described—a mix of race and class—would have great potential for addressing current economic grievances without generating resistance from people who oppose claims based on "old" grievances and who believe that they are being excluded from existing affirmative action programs. We also believe that such a program would unify people of different color, ethnicity, or gender rather than divide them into competing identity groups.

A FINAL NOTE ON ILLEGAL IMMIGRANTS

A current issue facing Americans that has great potential for dividing them into warring camps is the question of what to do regarding the estimated 10 to 12 million illegal immigrants currently in the United States. Most of these undocumented migrants are Mexican nationals, while some come from Central American nations. Most have come to the United States in search of a better life for themselves and their children, and Americans are divided about how welcoming we should be to people who have broken the law and what should be done. Let us exclude for the moment the views of groups that have their own agendas, like political groups that see immigrants as potential voters, union leaders who see them as workers who can be organized, and xenophobic or racist groups defending white supremacy. The remaining Americans who disagree on this issue tend to be divided into those claiming to be compassionate and generous versus those who are firm law abiders.

In order to move beyond the shouting and divided zealots on both sides, it will be necessary to identify a set of values that both sides embrace. For example, if both sides in the immigration debate can agree on endorsing the values of family and hard work, then it may be possible to develop legislation that both sides can endorse. Let's call it the Working Family Pathway to Citizenship Law and apply it to the current population of undocumented immigrants. Under this plan, if an illegal is married, has a family, has been employed in the United States for at least five years, has been paying Social Security, has children in local schools, and gets a reference from an employer, then s/he will be on the fast track to U.S. citizenship. At the other end of the spectrum, unmarried immigrants who have been in the United States a short time and have erratic employment records will be eligible for deportation. The law would list eligibility for citizenship according to the family-work conditions of the immigrant, with some becoming citizens and some deported.

We think that a Pathway to Citizenship Law that affirms certain shared values has a chance of unifying Americans who, on the one hand, want to be welcoming because they acknowledge that we were all immigrants once, with Americans who place high value on being law abiding and fair. Our approach here is the same one that we followed regarding affirmative action. The goal is to find common ground on divisive issues by identifying values that bring Americans together rather than those that divide. This is the only way in which a nation of people that has many identity groups can engender trust of each other.

6

Work, Family, and Caring

It has been said that an important measure of a country's level of civilization is the way in which its most vulnerable people are cared for. Generally, the most vulnerable are the children, the aged, the chronically ill, and those institutionalized. Additionally, even those who are independent and productive economically have needs for love and affection—caring broadly conceived.

Unfortunately, America does not measure up with respect to caring; indeed, some would say that there is a "crisis of caring" in our country.[1] In large part, this crisis comes from the persistence of an ideology of the private nuclear family in which the husband/father is the sole or main economic provider and the wife/mother is the dependent, unpaid, social-emotional provider for those in the family unit. The reality, however, is that today fewer and fewer people—indeed, only 23 percent —actually live in such families. The most common family type is that of married couples without children, where the couple has not yet had children or doesn't plan to have children, or where the children have grown up and left (28.5 percent). Similar in frequency are people living alone (26.4 percent). Other household types are male- or female-headed families in which relatives other than spouses or children live together (7.5 percent), female-headed (7.3 percent), unmarried couple households (5.3 percent), and male-headed single-parent families (1.7 percent).[2]

SHARING PAID WORK

At the turn of the twentieth century, women who were employed outside the home were largely single, widowed, relatively poor, and/or immigrants.

95

Their work was taking in laundry, marketing baked goods, working as do-
mestics in other people's homes, housing boarders, and factory work. For
married couples, work and family were integrated, with the nuclear family
being the work unit, first in the home and then in early factories. With the
development of technology within the factory system, husbands, wives, and
children were separated from one another and under the supervision of
others, often strangers. This led to considerable social concern and eventually to the shortening of the workday and work restrictions on women and
children who were relegated to educational institutions.

During the latter half of the twentieth century, however, women, including mothers of infants and young children, increasingly entered the paid
labor force. For instance, in 1900, only about 22 percent of women were in
the paid labor force. By 1970, 50 percent of wives with children between
ages of six and seventeen years were gainfully employed, and by 2005, that
figure had grown to 75 percent.[3] Those in the labor force include a broad
spectrum of women, cutting across social class, race and ethnicity, age, and
parental status. For instance, white women have a labor force participation
rate of 60 percent, almost as high as that of black women (62 percent), who
historically have been more likely to work for wages.[4] Moreover, women are
increasingly staying in the labor force throughout childbearing years, such
as 56 percent of married women with children under one year of age, and
they are staying for longer and longer years of their lives.

Child-development experts and the general public do not consider employed mothers problematic. For the wives themselves, benefits of employment include enhanced self-esteem, more power in the marital relationship,
greater economic independence, and a wider set of social relationships.

For husbands, some benefits from their wives' employment include being relieved of sole responsibility for the financial support of the family,
having more freedom to quit jobs or change jobs, more freedom to go to
school, having a spouse with whom to share ups and downs of their work
roles, having a happier spouse, and having increased potential to more
strongly bond with their children through active child care.

Moreover, a 2001 survey of women in general found that 90 percent
agree that a woman can be a good mother and have a successful career.[5]
Recent research concludes that mothers' employment does not cause
behavior problems in children.[6] Additionally, research on maternal employment during the child's first three years found no differences at age
twelve between the children whose mothers were employed versus not
employed in those early years of development.[7] One area of some concern is that children's lives may be becoming more tightly organized with
school, organized sports, chores, and accompanying parents on errands
rather than engaging in unstructured play or self-organized activities with
other children.

Recent research indicates no difference in cognitive development and psychological well being between children raised by homosexual parents and those raised by heterosexual parents. Children in homosexual families are no more likely to experience confusion about their own sexual orientation; the vast majority identify as heterosexual. They are more accepting of diversity and open to homosexuality and less gender-typed in their behavior. Lesbian coparents often have greater compatibility in terms of childrearing views and practices and a more equal division of caregiving responsibilities than either gay male coparents or heterosexual parents.[8]

Women tend to work in different types of jobs than men. The degree to which men and women are concentrated in occupations in which workers of one sex predominate is known as occupational sex segregation. This is measured by the dissimilarity index, the proportion of workers of one sex that would have to change to jobs in which members of their sex are underrepresented in order for the occupational distribution between the sexes to be fully balanced. The United States has a dissimilarity index of about thirty-eight, meaning that about 38 percent of its female labor force would have to change jobs in order to equalize their representation across occupations. Another way to measure occupational sex segregation is to look at the percentage of workers of each sex that holds a specific job. For example, in 2001, 97.6 percent of construction workers, 95.3 percent of mechanics, and 94.7 percent of truck drivers were male. On the other hand, 98.4 percent of secretaries, 93.1 percent of registered nurses, and 92.9 percent of bookkeepers were female.[9]

The extent of occupational sex segregation masks both industrywide and establishment sex segregation. Industry sex segregation is when women and men hold the same job title in a particular field or industry but actually perform different jobs. Women usually are concentrated in the lower-paying, lower-prestige specialties within the occupation. For example, among real estate agents, women are more often in residential home sales while men are in the more profitable commercial real estate sales.

Establishment sex segregation is when women and men hold the same job title at an individual establishment or company but actually do different jobs. For example, in a law firm, women often are concentrated in family law, while men are likely to be in the more lucrative corporate and commercial law.

Occupational sex segregation, then, results in women generally working mostly with other women instead of with men. The result is that even full-time work in women's fields is remunerated at lower salaries, offers limited upward mobility ("glass ceiling"), seldom has union protection, and generally does not come with access to pensions or prestige.

And there are other ways in which women are not welcomed and nurtured in the work world. If they are few in number in the workplace compared with the number of men there, they are likely to be treated in stereotypical ways, as representatives of their category, rather than as individuals. They are more closely scrutinized by others, and they are treated as outsiders.

Many women also experience sexual harassment from men in the workplace. This is defined as any unwanted leers, comments, suggestions, or physical contact of a sexual nature, as well as unwelcome requests for sexual favors. Research indicates that from 42 percent to 88 percent of women workers experience sexual harassment at some point during their work lives.[10]

Then there is the wage gap, the difference in earnings between men and women. The size of the gap varies, depending on occupation, and tends to be greater in the higher-paying occupations, such as physicians. The size of the gap also is related to occupational specialty and practice setting. Additionally, the gender wage gap is due to different work patterns; namely, women having fewer years of work experience, having fewer hours of work per year, being less likely to work full time, and leaving the labor force for longer periods than men's work patterns. Women's work patterns are often adapted to care for their children or others.[11] It is debatable the extent to which women freely choose to invest less in employment outside the home (human capital theory) versus having to take the occupational opportunities available to them. The unexplained part of the gap is usually assumed to result from discrimination.

Overall, in 2001, African American women earned 84.4 percent of what white women earned; Hispanic women earned just 74.7 percent of what white women earned. African American men earned 74.7 percent of what white men earned; whereas, Hispanic men earned only 62.2 percent of what white men earned.[12]

Due in part to the feminist and civil rights movements in the 1960s, the federal government acted to make sex discrimination in employment illegal. First came Title VII of the 1964 Civil Rights Act, which forbids discrimination in hiring, benefits, and other personnel decisions, such as promotions or layoffs, on the basis of sex, race, color, national origin, or religion, by employers of fifteen or more employees. This act has been implemented and enforced by the Equal Employment Opportunity Commission, which can bring suit on behalf of an employee or class of employees who have been discriminated against by their employer.

Second is Executive Order 11246, which was amended in 1968 to outlaw sex discrimination as well as discrimination based on race, color, national origin, and religion by employers who hold federal contracts. It requires employers to take affirmative action to recruit, train, and promote women and minorities. Contractor compliance has been monitored by the Office of Federal Contract Compliance in the Department of Labor, as well as the U.S. Department of Justice. The effects of Title VII and Executive Order 11246 have been limited by their complexity, which gives judges considerable discretion, and by political change in the presidency and U.S. Supreme Court.

Discriminatory pay policies have been attacked directly by the Equal Pay Act of 1963. It prohibits employers from paying employees of one sex more than employees of the opposite sex when their employees are engaged in work that requires equal skill, effort, and responsibility and that is performed under similar working conditions. Unequal pay is permitted if the difference is based on employees' relative seniority, merit, the quantity or quality of their production, or "any other factor other than sex" such as profitability of their work.[13] The benefits of this act are limited, however, because men and women are largely segregated into different jobs, and predominantly female jobs are systematically devalued.[14]

As a result, women workers and others have increasingly called for "comparable worth"; that is, equal pay for different jobs of similar value in terms of skill, effort, responsibility, and working conditions. In general, the courts have not looked favorably on comparable worth because they do not wish "to punish employers who rely on the market in setting wages . . . and do not wish to become involved in evaluating the worth of different jobs." However, numerous states and local jurisdictions have adopted comparable worth policies.[15]

Steinberg and Cook conducted a broader view of what it would take to close the gender gap in wages:

> Equal employment requires more than guaranteeing the right to equal access, the right to equal opportunity for promotion, or the right to equal pay for equal work, or even comparable worth. Additionally, it warrants a broader policy orientation encompassing social welfare laws that assume equality within the family; wide-spread use of alternative work arrangements that accommodate the complexities of family life within two-career families; and a rejuvenated union movement, with female leadership more active at work sites in defending the rights of women workers. Social welfare laws, family policy, and government services must create incentives toward a more equal division of responsibilities for family and household tasks between men and women. Increasing child care facilities, as well as maintaining programs to care for the elderly, would help alleviate some of the more pressing demands made on adults in families . . . This also means that tax policy, social security laws, and pension programs must be amended to make government incentives to family life consistent with a family structure in which husbands and wives are equal partners.[16]

Families turned to the wife as a second earner increasingly in the 1970s when there was a decline of men's jobs, especially blue-collar jobs, and men's earnings, and uncertainty in sectors that had been doing relatively well. Women became less certain about being out of the labor force and dependent on a husband's earnings as the divorce rate grew. Also, the women's movement reemerged, pushing for anti-sex-discrimination laws that opened educational and occupational opportunities to women. The majority of married women had become employed by 1979. But this led to social concern once again, this time to reintegrate work and family.

The historical change from an agrarian economy in which the household was the central economic unit to a capitalist market structure made family caregiving problematic, as it ended worker autonomy and control over the incompatibility between home work and market production. Children increasingly became economic and social costs that mothers especially, not communities or employers, bore. At the same time that demands on families to raise well-rounded children were increasing, demands and rewards for market work were similarly increasing. As automation eliminated human physical labor and globalization made labor cheap, workers were encouraged to invest even more in a 24/7 economy.

SHARING UNPAID HOME WORK

So, who is providing the care for America's homes and children? One possibility is that since women now shoulder both economic provider and caretaker roles, the same could obtain for men. Husbands of employed wives do participate in more of the unpaid home work than husbands whose wives are not employed. Women have reduced their hours in housework from forty hours per week in 1965 to twenty-seven hours per week in 1999, while men have only increased their housework time from twelve hours in 1965 to sixteen hours per week in 1999.[17] Although housework is socially and economically necessary work, it is not considered "real" work, not even by many of the women who have primary responsibility for doing it. This is because it is unspecialized, it is repetitive and never fully finished, it has no fixed work schedule, it is privatized, it is involved with feelings of love and care, and probably most importantly, it is unpaid.

Also, the tasks that men typically perform are different from those done by wives. Women tend to do chores that must be done on a daily basis, such as cleaning and cooking families' meals at least once or twice a day, every day. Husbands tend to participate in chores that need to be done only occasionally and can be done at their convenience, such as mowing the lawn and making minor repairs around the house.

Some men, especially young men, are choosing less competitive careers to spend more time with their families. Indeed, a small minority of men have given up employment to stay home to care for the house and family while their wives work ("househusbands"). However, such men may have to deal with challenges to their masculinity, resentment from co-workers, and disapproval from employers who believe that employees should not allow family responsibilities to interfere with labor-force involvement. This puts a brake on the extent to which men take advantage of family-friendly benefits that are theoretically available (e.g., paternity leave for professional and managerial employees).

Women are responsible not only for most housework but also for the bulk of child care. So, in general the overall amount of home work that husbands perform does not approximate that done by wives, which is called a "second shift" of unpaid work that amounts to an extra month of work each year.[18]

The addition of children to a household increases household chores, financial pressures, and stress for the couple, particularly mothers. Over the past thirty years, there has been increased involvement of fathers in child care, but mothers still participate in much more primary child care—bathing, changing clothes, feeding—than fathers. Mothers also participate in more of the "mental work" associated with child care—worrying, seeking advice and information involved in childrearing. Fathers are least involved when their children are infants and become more involved as the children grow up, particularly in recreational or academic activities, not primary care.

An expectation—by employers, co-workers, and many men themselves—that men's chief responsibility as a husband/father is as breadwinner underlies the unequal division of labor in the home. Mothers as caregivers could be considered to have an advantage in bonding closely with their children and being the "kin keepers" or links across generations of the family. Disadvantages for mothers include lost autonomy, less time and ability to pursue interests outside the home, including paid work and leisure activities. Significantly, women's caregiving work is not covered by Social Security because it is not paid labor, or by unemployment or workmen's compensation. In the event of divorce, moreover, courts seldom count the economic contributions of caregivers and place the bulk of childrearing costs on the divorced mothers.[19]

Mothers may have not only child care responsibilities but also caregiving to elderly parents ("sandwich generation"). And the number of individuals in this sandwich generation will increase for several reasons. For one thing, the over-eighty-five group, who are most likely to be frail and in need of care, is the fastest growing segment of the American population. The care that they will increasingly need, moreover, is to manage long-term chronic, not acute, illnesses, such as Alzheimer's. And there are fewer adult siblings to help look after elderly parents because the latter had fewer children than the elderly in previous generations. The adult children generally are committed to caring for their elderly parents and institutionalize them only as a last resort. There are some benefits of caregiving, such as enhanced self-esteem and a closer relationship to the dependent person. On the other hand, the effort, sacrifice, and decision-making on the part of the caretaker may lead to an emotional toll—feeling guilt for not doing enough, resentment from feeling burdened, and exhaustion from constant care demands. Some strain can be relieved from home health care in which an employee provides such services as bathing and dressing the parent and supervising medication. Also, there may be community services such as Meals on Wheels to assist elderly persons who are homebound and cannot cook for themselves anymore.

Often as a last resort, those in the sandwich generation decide to put an aged parent, usually their mother, in some form of long-term care such as a nursing home. Such a decision depends importantly on cost. Medicare typically does not pay for long-term nursing care, leaving the middle-aged child and the elderly parent to pay costs. It is only after most of the elder's funds have been depleted that Medicaid will pay for the cost of care. Other considerations are the level of care needed by the elderly parent, the temperament of the parent, the sense of responsibility of the adult child, the length of time for providing care, and the privacy needs of the caregivers.

Not only does the middle-aged child often care for her elderly parents but also some minor-aged children care for their parents ("parentification"). Situations in which children become their parents' caretakers include when parents have become chronically ill, chemically dependent, mentally ill, incapacitated after a divorce or widowhood, or socially isolated or incapacitated. Parentification may become a normative part of childhood when children only temporarily take care of a parent, e.g., after surgery or during an illness. Parentification is considered destructive when the circumstances become extreme and long-term and the responsibilities that children carry are age-inappropriate. Some care-related consequences of parentification for the children include the children's delay in taking on the caretaking that comes with marriage; the acquisition of certain personality characteristics, such as feelings of excessive responsibility for others that make it difficult to set limits with others or to concentrate on their own needs; the child's seeking as adult partners people who they can be caretakers for; and taking jobs where they can physically or emotionally take care of people, as in nursing.

In part, the imbalance in doing home work between spouses is due to the great difficulty of combining employment with unpaid caregiving for men as well as women in the United States. Usually the workplace is not supportive of employees with family responsibilities. Caring for newborn and young children requires rapt attention during the child's waking hours, which is incompatible even with home-based employment settings for the small minority of workers whose jobs permit such flexibility. And work start times conflict with school start times, and work hours typically extend beyond the end-of-school day, not to mention during school holidays throughout the year and during summers. Relatively few employers provide on-site, full-day day care for infants and young children, leaving parents to try to find their own solutions.

WORK-FAMILY SPILLOVER

Work affects people's home life by absorbing time and energy and impinging on their psychological states. Conversely, the demands of home lives impinge on concentration, energy, and/or availability at work. These relationships between paid work and family life are called "spillover." Overall, both women and men experience greater job-to-home spillover than home-to-job spillover. Women experience higher levels of job-to-home spillover than do men, and having a partner and children increases negative spillover for women but usually not for men. Time pressures on the job and long work hours have the most job-to-home spillover for both women and men.

The U.S. economy has been called the "greedy institution" because of the large amount of time required of workers. One view of how much time Americans spend at work focuses on the amount of time that dual-earner couples jointly work instead of the individual earner's time. U.S. Census data show that the family transformation from single (male) earner to dual-earner couples in which wives work accounts for most of the growth in working time. Additionally, there is an increasing segment of the population working extremely long hours, namely, couples who are highly educated and in high-profile professional and managerial occupations. As noted above, women's increased work has not been accompanied by a corresponding increase in fathers' home work, thus producing a time squeeze.

Time Wars

Despite rising divorce rates, as mentioned above, women may scale back their paid work to part time or quit work altogether. Also, the wife may insist that the husband and their children participate in housework. She may lower her standards for cleanliness and reduce her food preparation time. Two-earner couples may hire household help and child care help.

Dual-earner couples, especially those with children, continually struggle to find new ways to accommodate their work and family schedules. They make daily and weekly assignments of who is going to take or pick up the children from day care or from school. They partner with friends and co-workers about carpooling and child pickup pooling. They use their cell phones to give their child care providers a mile-by-mile update on exactly where they are on their trip from work to the child care facility. Husbands and wives often have to renegotiate daily plans because of a change in work schedules. And there is always the unanticipated event like a family illness that throws a monkey wrench into the family schedule.

Couples may also try to solve the child care problem by shift work, in which one parent works during the day and the other parent works the evening or night shift so that one parent can always be with the children. The routine scheduling problems of dual earners who work normal-day schedules are even more complicated when one or both parents work a nonroutine schedule; that is, something other than 8:00 a.m. to 5:00 p.m. on Monday through Friday. In the workplace today there are about 15 to 20 million workers who do shift work. If they work eight-hour shifts, they may work 4:00 p.m. to 12:00 p.m., or 12:00 p.m. to 8:00 a.m.; if they are on twelve-hour shifts, it may be 7:00 a.m. to 7:00 p.m. or 7:00 p.m. to 7:00 a.m. These shifts may be fixed where a worker has the same pattern all year, or they may be rotating where a worker works one month on the evening shift and then rotates to one month on the night shift.[20] Some workers choose shift work because it accommodates their family needs. Consider the following comments from two shift workers:

> I am content with my work schedule. My wife works nights and I work days, so we don't have to purchase child care for our baby. She hates working nights but it's all we can do for now. I wish she didn't have to work but in today's times that's unrealistic.

> I work 12-hour nights so I can take my children to school and pick them up. This only allows me five hours of sleep on the days that I work. Which means I try to sleep more on my days off, which I find difficult to do. I do work nights by choice, because my wife's schedule does not allow her to be there for the children, and I do not trust anyone with my children.

Although some workers choose shift work to accommodate family schedules, others report that their family life is under considerable stress. Consider the following comments from dual-earner families with one spouse doing shift work:

> Working five days a week from 8:00 a.m. to 5:00 p.m. means that I leave for work only a few minutes after my husband gets home in the morning. When my husband is having days off during my work week, I am resentful. He is able to enjoy golf and fishing while I am at work. When my husband has weekends off, our home is more harmonious, but when he works weekends, we never see each other and I become depressed.

> My husband's work schedule makes me feel as though I have a roommate more than a spouse. The majority of time we sleep at different times, visit our

families separately, and make plans on our own. We often communicate by leaving notes.

> Because of my schedule, my wife and I have been discussing divorce. Because of my job and hers, we spend nearly no time together at all. She works days, usually 7:00 a.m. to 4:00 p.m. I don't get home until 7:30 a.m., then I usually sleep until 4:30 p.m. or 5:00 p.m., and I leave for work around 6:00 p.m. We see each other about eight to ten hours a week.[21]

Adjusting work schedules for shift workers in order to have more family-friendly schedules presents a challenge to both employers and to workers. The authors once conducted a research project in a shift-work manufacturing plant that employed about 900 workers. During our time there, management and the union discussed a plan that might give younger workers more flexibility in their work schedules. In this plant, seniority rules determined shift assignments, so that new hires who were younger men and women with family responsibilities usually were assigned to the evening and night shifts. The plan under discussion would allow any worker to reduce his/her workday, week, month, or year by 20 percent. This meant that a parent could get off work early each day in order to accommodate a family need, or a parent could take time off during the summer months when children were not in school. The time off would be unpaid, but it would not affect other employee benefits.

Discussions about the proposed new policy took place over a year and always ran into resistance from one side or the other. Management agreed to consider the plan if they could employ temporary workers to fill in for workers who took advantage of the 20 percent reduction option. The union opposed this idea because using temporary nonunion workers would be a violation of union policy. Management countered with a proposal to require mandatory overtime from workers to fill in for those on family leave. The union opposed this idea because the current contract allowed only for voluntary overtime.

Although both management and the union held serious discussions about a more family-friendly schedule, an agreement was not achieved because of management's concern about meeting production schedules and union concern about avoiding new rules that might harm the union. Both sides participated in discussions in good faith, but both had needs that they were not willing to compromise. In short, there may be limits to how far management or workers are willing to go in order to accommodate the needs of younger workers with family responsibilities.

Dual-career couples in which both spouses pursue full-time, demanding professional and managerial work may have travel requirements that necessitate overnight child care. Finding such dependable household help is possible only to the extent that there is a labor pool of low-paid workers. Moreover, upward career mobility may require geographical mobility, which may make for a trailing spouse who relocates to accommodate the other spouse's career. As an alternative, some couples live apart as commuter marriages. Such an arrangement seems to work better for established partners with a history of shared time, when there are no dependent children, and when couples get together frequently. In general, commuters are less satisfied with their partner and family life than with their work life. A Gallup Poll in 2003 found that almost half —48 percent—of American adults in general felt that they had too little time to do what they wanted to do.[22] Both men and women spent very little time, about twenty minutes per day on average, in wider community activities; i.e., organizational, civic, and religious activities.[23]

Relatively privileged married women can scale back their work to forgo a serious career and/or take a "mommy track" or part-time work in an effort to combine work with family responsibilities. They may leave the labor force altogether for the time that their children are young but plan on reentering at a later date. Reentry, however, may have its problems; notably, inability to get full-time work and lost earning capacity. They also lose important benefits and become more dependent on the good will of husbands.

Parenting without Partners

There is a growing number of single women-headed households with children who often live in poverty. In 2000, some 5 percent of married couple families lived in poverty in contrast to 10 percent of single-father families and 25 percent of single-mother families.[24] Some parents are little more than children themselves. The United States has one of the highest rates of births to single teen mothers among Western industrialized countries. Fortunately, the rate of teen pregnancy and childbirth in the United States has declined steadily since 1960. There were 89.1 pregnancies/1,000 girls aged 15 to 19 in 1960 compared with 51.1 pregnancies/1,000 girls aged 15 to 19 in 1998.[25] The decline in teen pregnancies is thought to be due to there being more comprehensive sex education in the schools, teens having sexual intercourse less, and those teens having intercourse being more likely to use contraception in order to avoid contracting HIV/AIDS as well as becoming pregnant. Motivation to abstain from sex or to use contraceptives appears to be promoted by the availability of opportunities besides parenthood for achieving status and self-esteem.

The teen birth rate for racial and ethnic minorities remains high—85.4 births/1,000 African American girls aged 15 to 19 and 93.6 births/1,000 Hispanic girls aged 15 to 19 in l998.[26] These high rates have been linked to the higher rate of poverty and lower levels of academic success among minority girls. Babies born to teen mothers, moreover, are more likely to be premature or have low birth weight; grow up in poverty; have serious health problems; have difficulty in school; enter the criminal justice system if they are boys; and become mothers themselves if they are girls.[27]

Mothers are also single in part due to widowhood, although the percent of single-parent families in which the parent is widowed has declined since 1970. Widowed women outnumber widowed men because men have higher mortality rates and are more likely to remarry than widowed women. Women are far more likely than men to experience financial difficulties during widowhood for several reasons: women traditionally have had shorter and less stable employment histories than men; they earn less, on average, than men, which limits their Social Security and asset accumulation; and they are less likely than men to have been employed in occupations that carry fringe benefits such as pensions. Nonwhite women are especially likely to have a negative financial impact from widowhood.

The most common way in which women and men become single is through divorce. In 2003 the crude divorce rate was 3.8 divorces per 1,000 population. Another way of looking at divorce is that current estimates suggest that about 40 percent of those married in the past two decades will divorce.[28] About 25 percent of university students have parents who are divorced. Women with limited education and income and who marry early in life have less stable marriages.

Although research on single fathers is limited, it appears that single fathers receive more support from friends, relatives, and neighbors than single mothers receive. Single fathers' most common complaint is that their social lives and careers become more restrained by parenting demands and that they are treated as less-competent parents.

Single mothers have more constraints in balancing work with children because the jobs they hold often have less flexible work schedules and low salaries. Their main problem is lack of money. Why are single divorced women usually more in need of money than single divorced men? Some observers attribute this to no-fault divorce laws in which spousal support awards are limited; that is, the courts try to treat divorcing spouses as equals when, in fact, the wife usually has fewer financial resources in terms of wages, adequate social welfare, and child support from the father.

SOLUTIONS IN OTHER COUNTRIES
VERSUS THE UNITED STATES

Clearly, both single and dual-earner parents face increasing pressures at work and at home and need assistance in meeting work and family responsibilities. Many countries, both developing and developed economically, provide workers assistance in terms of parental leave following the birth of a child and/or government-subsidized child care services. More than thirty developing countries provide paid infant-care leave. Additionally, several industrialized countries provide parental leave benefits, and it applies for fathers as well as mothers. In Finland, for example, parents have a year of fully paid leave.[29] With respect to child care, in Finland parents can choose between a subsidy to help pay for in-home care or a guaranteed, heavily subsidized place in a child care center.

In contrast to the industrialized nations discussed above, in the United States there is no paid parental-leave policy, or family allowances, child care services, housing subsidies, or universal health care coverage. Instead, there is some legal recourse for pregnancy discrimination provided by the federal Pregnancy Discrimination Act of 1978, which forbids employers to fire, demote, or penalize a pregnant employee. This law pertains only to employers with more than fifteen workers, although some state laws extend this protection to smaller companies, including those with as few as four employees. The law is not always followed, however; between 1996 and 2000, for example, almost 5 percent of women reported being laid off while pregnant or within twelve weeks after giving birth.[30]

In 1993 the U.S. Congress passed the Family and Medical Leave Act (FMLA), which allows eligible employees to take up to twelve weeks of unpaid annual leave, with continuation of health benefits, for three situations: after the birth or adoption of a child and to care for a newborn; to care for a seriously sick spouse, child, or parent; or to recover from their own illnesses that prevent them from working. An employee is eligible for leave only if s/he has worked at least 1,250 hours during a twelve-month period at a company that employs at least fifty people. A company may require or allow employees to apply paid vacation and sick leave to the twelve weeks of family leave, but the company does not have to pay workers who take leave.

To no longer lose jobs because of childbirth, sickness, or parental leave is certainly a benefit to American workers. Additionally, all but the top-level employees are guaranteed the same job or an equivalent job when they return. Also, in 2000 about 40 percent of women had some paid leave, which most companies funded through a general temporary disability insurance plan.[31]

Limitations to the FMLA are that it provides only for twelve weeks of unpaid leave, which many employees simply cannot afford to take; it does not cover small companies, where 60 percent of employees work; it covers only major illnesses; there are employer-employee disputes over what constitutes "equivalent" jobs; and almost one-third of eligible employers offer fewer than twelve weeks of unpaid leave, in violation of the FMLA.[32]

On the other hand, the United States is growing stronger with respect to child support policy. This began in 1950 when federal legislation was enacted to enforce child-support payment. A 1975 act created the bureaucracy to enforce private child-support obligations. From 1976 to 1977, mothers' likelihood of actually receiving child support increased barely from 36 percent to 42 percent.

A 1984 law requires states to adopt guidelines that the courts can use to determine such obligations. Moreover, it requires states to withhold pay from the wages and other income of noncustodial parents who have not made their child-support payments. A 1988 act requires judges to provide a written justification if they violate state guidelines. It also instructs states to review and update child-support awards every three years.

Some corporations, especially large ones, have policies designed to assist parents of young children. These include support groups for employed parents, workplace seminars and counseling programs, parental or family leaves, subsidies for child care services or child care locator services, sick-child care, and even on-site child care centers. Perhaps most common are policies allowing flexible scheduling, such as flextime in which there are flexible starting and ending times, with required core hours. Also, some employers permit job sharing in which two people share one position. Other flexible scheduling policies include working at home or telecommuting, compressed workweeks in which an employee is allowed to concentrate the workweek into three or four longer days, and personal days off.

Working at home either for oneself or for an employer increased 55 percent between 1990 and 2000. In 2004, 15 percent of workers were home-based as part of their primary job, and one-third of them were self-employed. Two-thirds were managerial or professional employees, and about half are women. Some home-based work involves piecework, such as the assembly of medical kits, circuit boards, jewelry, and some textile work. Other home-based work includes the direct selling of cosmetics, kitchenware, etc., as well as an independent contractor to handle customer service calls. While women say that they work at home in order to try to minimize conflicts with housework and child care, they also report problems with interruptions and tension between career advancement, which requires putting in long hours, and family time.

The small amount of societal assistance with child care means that employed parents, especially mothers, then, must cobble together various caregiving alternatives, such as extranuclear family kin. The major one is for-profit day care. Guidelines for high-quality day care have been developed by the American Academy of Pediatrics and include the following: low child-to-staff ratio; stable staff; a well-trained staff; staff sensitive to cultural diversity; staff with warm personalities and interpersonal sensitivity; staff who give age-appropriate attention to children and age-appropriate and stimulating activities and play spaces for children; staff who are responsive to children and interact with them, rather than provide only custodial care or allow lots of TV watching; staff who do not use physical punishment for handling minor behavior problems that arise with children; and staff who welcome parental involvement.[33]

Such high-quality care is limited in most communities and often not affordable for many when it is available. More typically this leaves care in institutional settings of questionable merit, usually performed by women with limited preparation for child care, earning low wages and subject to high turnover. Pressures to cut costs, government regulations, and bureaucratization are some of the factors that compromise such care, especially social and emotional caregiving, which children need.

As noted earlier, the United States has no national child care program. Moreover, only 7 percent of employers with fifty or more employees provide child care at or near the workplace; and at those who do, the costs are too high for many low-wage workers.[34]

Arrangements that mothers make for child care depend on availability of care, costs, hours of operation of the programs, and race/ethnicity. For about 15 percent of children aged five to fourteen, almost double since the 1970s, this means self-care ("latchkey") after school until an adult comes home. Nearly twice the white five- to fourteen-year-olds compared to African American and Latino children are latchkey kids to some extent. It is questionable to what extent five- to nine-year-olds are able to deal with household emergencies that may occur. Latino parents are more likely to depend on relatives other than the parents, while African American parents are more likely to use child care centers.

Economic dependency from low incomes and poverty leads many women to remain living with even abusive partners and spouses and children to risk abuse at home or in foster homes. Children of very young ages, females, minorities, and those from unwanted or unplanned pregnancies are at high risk of neglect and abuse. Mothers are more likely than fathers to abuse children, possibly because of the greater contact with them. Stepfathers and boyfriends of single mothers are also more likely than fathers to abuse children. Traumatic effects of childhood abuse may continue into adulthood.

Based on survey data from large, representative samples of heterosexual couples, about 12 percent of adult intimates experience some form of physical abuse from their partners out of every 1,000 couples; and 122 wives and 124 husbands of every 1,000 couples are assaulted by their spouse.[35] The less common and more extreme violence that causes serious injury or even death is usually committed by men against women. Battered women seldom have educational or employment opportunities that would facilitate their leaving an abusive spouse.

In 1994 the federal Violence Against Women Act was passed. It provides for funding for battered women's shelters and programs, a mandate for harsher penalties for battering, and a provision that makes crossing state lines in pursuit of a fleeing partner a federal offense. Another important societal strategy for change would be to reduce violence-provoking stress by reducing poverty and unemployment and providing educational opportunities for all.

UNEMPLOYMENT AND FAMILIES

Just as heavy work demands conflict with family responsibilities, so is unemployment from restructuring and downsizing a major source of worker stress. The economic strain involves financial concerns and worry, adjustments to changes in income, and feelings of economic insecurity. With increases in economic strain come increases in infant mortality, alcoholism, family abuse, homicide, suicide, and admissions to psychiatric institutions and prisons.[36] Economic strain is also related to lower levels of marital satisfaction as a result of financial conflict, the husband's psychological instability, and marital tensions. The families that are hardest hit by unemployment are single-parent families headed by women, African American and Latino families, and young families. Workers in female-headed and minority families tend to remain unemployed longer than other types of families. And young families with preschool children often lack the seniority, experience, and skills to regain employment quickly. So, economic downturns affect families in the early years of childbearing and childrearing the most, driving many into poverty and even homelessness, the topics of the next chapter.

In sum, the family's role in caregiving has evolved with industrialization and deindustrialization. While women responded to the increased demand for their paid labor, there was no corresponding societal response to the need for support for unpaid labor, especially the care of children. And with increases in involuntary unemployment, there is increased need for social supports for displaced workers and their families. Children are America's future, and their nurturance warrants priority—with increased money, time, and laws and policies dedicated to reintegrating work and family spheres of life.

7

Forgotten Americans: The Poor, Homeless, Aged, and Incarcerated

Compromised care is characteristic not only of much child care, as discussed in chapter 6, but also care of the poor, homeless, aged, and incarcerated. At an earlier time, families had more responsibility for care of others in the community, whereas now institutional care and government programs are more common and necessary.

POVERTY

Poverty underlies many problems experienced by a large number of Americans. It is a paradox that in the richest country in the developed world, 34.6 million or 12.1 percent of Americans live in poverty. Among African Americans, 24.4 percent live in poverty; Hispanics, 21.9 percent; and Asian Americans, 10.1 percent. That means that they lack access to basic needs such as food, clothing, shelter, health care, and necessities for successful work such as a decent education and access to means of transportation.[1]

In 2007 the official poverty threshold was $20,630 for a family of four (two adults and two children). It was $10,200 for one person; $13,690 for two; and $17,170 for a family of three. This refers to gross earnings before taxes, unadjusted for differences in costs of living among different places, and based on the assumption that families need only three times expenditures for their basic food needs. It does not include either direct income or in-kind income from public assistance.

Who are the American poor? They are children under the age of eighteen, especially children of color, and especially those living in certain states. A recent study of states using ten indicators of child well-being shows how the top state compares to the bottom state.[2] With respect to the indicator of percent of children living in poverty, in the bottom state of Mississippi, the child poverty rate (30 percent) is three times greater than in the top state of Maryland (10 percent). In 1999, one in six children, overall, 16.6 percent, lived in poverty. One in seven, 14.2 percent, lack health care; a child in Texas is five times as likely to be uninsured (21.2 percent) as a child in Rhode Island (4.2 percent). This means they do not receive recommended preventive health care visits and immunizations.

These children live largely in poor families who work but do not make enough income to put them above the poverty line. This is tied to the decline of high-wage jobs and the growth of jobs considered to be low wage. It is also linked to the growing income and wealth inequality that is tearing the American society apart. A study by the National Commission on Children concluded that America was failing many of its children:

> Although many children grow up healthy and happy in strong, stable families, far too many do not. They are children whose parents are too stressed and busy to provide caring attention and guidance. They are children who grow up without the material support and personal involvement of their mothers and fathers. They are children who are poor, whose families cannot adequately feed and clothe them, and provide safe, secure homes. They are children who are victims of abuse and neglect at the hands of adults they love and trust, as well as those they don't even know. They are children who are born too early and too small, who face a lifetime of chronic illness and disability. They are children who enter school ill-prepared for the rigors of learning, who fail to develop the skills and attitudes needed to get good jobs and become responsible members of adult society. They are children who lack hope for what their lives can become, who believe they have little to lose by dropping out of school, having a baby as an unmarried teenager, committing violent crimes, or taking their own lives.[3]

SINGLE MOTHERS

The poor are also women, especially women of color and some elderly. Women's poverty is directly related to their experience in the labor force: differences from men in remuneration rates for comparable levels of education, occupational segregation into low-wage jobs, and discrimination. In 2006 women who worked full time earned $0.81 for every dollar earned by men. While the extent to which women and men work in different jobs declined from 1960 to 1990, women and men continue to be segregated at work. For example, in 2005, some 22 percent of women worked in office and administrative support, compared to only 6 percent of men.[4] Women dominate lower-wage, caregiving occupations such as nursery school and kindergarten teachers, registered nurses, librarians, social workers, elementary schoolteachers, and dieticians.

Households headed by single mothers are particularly likely to live at poverty level, and the number of such households headed by single mothers under age twenty-five is expected to increase from 831,000 in 1995 to 1.2 million in 2010.[5] African Americans have significantly higher numbers of never-married single mothers than do other groups. Looked at in terms of births, each year 1 million children are born to unwed parents. The percent of all births to unmarried women was only 4 to 5 percent of all births from 1940 until the early 1960s. In 1980 this rose to 18 percent, and after a decline in the 1990s, it rose to an all-time high of 39 percent in 2005.

Although child abuse occurs in families of all socioeconomic levels, it is reported more frequently among poor and nonwhite families than among middle- and upper-class white families. Indeed, families below the poverty line have three times the rate of severe violence to children. While differences in rates may be due in part to differences in reporting, experts believe there are also real differences. Parental stress is the most offered explanation. Another circumstance related to child maltreatment is a mother's cohabiting with her boyfriend, who is more likely than a child's male relative to abuse the child.

In the 1990s and early 2000s, rates of child physical abuse and child sexual abuse declined. Based on state reports in 2005, some 63 percent of reported cases of child maltreatment were of neglect, 17 percent of physical abuse, 9 percent of sexual abuse, 7 percent of psychological abuse, and 2 percent of medical neglect. The remainder of cases included multiple factors or unspecified abuse.[6]

A disproportionately high percent of children living below or near the poverty level are foster children. In foster care, a child is taken into temporary or permanent custody by state or county officials because they have determined that a child is being abused or neglected. Some foster care occurs in group homes for several children who are cared for by paid professionals who live elsewhere. Much of foster care takes place in a trained and licensed foster parent's home. Since the 1980s, some foster care is with biological relatives of children in their homes. Unfortunately, a factor associated with child abuse and neglect is that the children are foster children.

Measures taken by the government can improve the lives of mothers and children in single-parent homes. In the 1960s there were massive social programs known as the "war on poverty" that cut the poverty rate almost in half. Nearly 13 million people received Aid to Families with Dependent Children (AFDC), 27 million more received food stamps, about 6.2 million children received free school breakfasts, and 7.2 million pregnant women, infants, and children under two years of age participated in supplemental food programs known as the Women, Infants, and Children Program (WIC).

Relatively few of those who fall below the poverty line are there permanently; rather, they tend to be there for periods of time. About one-fourth of the American population receives welfare assistance at one time or another, and about one-half of American children experience a poverty period at least once during their childhood.

In the 1990s the war on poverty became a "war on welfare" as poverty ceased being viewed as a structural feature of our society and the poor were viewed as being to blame for their own poverty, undeserving of assistance. In 1996, under then President Clinton, the law converted AFDC to a block grant for a set amount to states, called Temporary Assistance to Needy Families (TANF). There is a five-year lifetime limit on benefits for welfare recipients. After two years of benefits, moreover, recipients are required to do one of three things: to work, to enroll in on-the-job or vocational train-ing, or to do community service. If the unmarried mothers are younger than age eighteen, they must reside with an adult and attend school to receive benefits. States could set eligibility rules and determine how participants could meet work requirements. Amounts of financial assistance also varied among the states; for example, thirteen states have a maximum TANF ben-efit of under $300/month, whereas six states allow $600 and above.

For a number of reasons, including being ineligible for welfare assistance, the number of welfare recipients nationwide dropped markedly. In 2004, about one-third of adults on welfare were working. Many former recipients are working at low-wage jobs that cause them hardships, such as skipping meals for financial reasons, postponing needed medical care, and being unable to pay their rent, mortgage, or utility bills.[7]

Just above those in poverty officially are over 50 million Americans, includ-ing 20 percent of the country's children, who are "near poor" or members of what Newman and Chen call the "missing class."[8] Their incomes put them above the poverty line but well below the middle class. They are families with two parents and two children who live on between $20,000 and $40,000 a year. This disqualifies them for almost all public subsidies, including health care via Medicaid, and leaves them unable to be self-sufficient.

A growing fringe-economy sector is taking advantage of the growing part of the U.S. population who are poor and economically insecure. This refers to a variety of businesses that charge excessive interest rates, extremely high fees, or exorbitant prices for goods or services. Some of these businesses are payday lenders, check-cashers, pawnshops, tax refund lenders, rent-to-own stores, and "buy-here/pay-here" used car lots. The large amounts of capital to fund the fringe-economy corporations is coming increasingly from mainstream financial institutions, such as Wells Fargo and JPMorgan Chase Bank.[9]

This compares with the federal government providing what may be called "corporate welfare"—$150 billion in 2002 in direct subsidies to the shipping, railroad, and airline industries, along with exporters of iron, steel, textiles, paper, and other products. Taxpayers fund corporate welfare, leaving less money for financial assistance to poor, low-income, and even middle-class families.[10]

THE HOMELESS

Among the Americans living in poverty are an estimated 750,000 people who are homeless on any given night, with 20 percent of them considered chronically homeless. These figures come from annual surveys, conducted since 2005, by approximately 4,000 communities nationwide.[11] The surveys are coordinated to avoid double-counting the itinerant homeless. Nevertheless, it is difficult to get a handle on the magnitude of the homeless, who by definition live in cars, boxes, makeshift shelters, and with relatives and friends from time to time.

Who exactly are the homeless in America? The fastest growing group of homeless people is families, with families with children accounting for 40 percent of the homeless. This is up from 34 percent in the late 1990s. Eighty-four percent of the children live in single-mother families. Their plight is exemplified by the situation of a homeless, single-mother family with three children living in her car and parking somewhere different each night so no one would notice them. Children in homeless families are sometimes instructed to tell anyone who asks about their residence that they are staying with friends.[12]

Why is there homelessness among American families? There are a number of factors including poverty, discussed above, as well as lack of education, lack of marketable skills, unemployment, domestic violence (discussed in chapter 6), substance abuse, lack of affordable housing, and the inability of relatives and friends to provide social and economic support during crises. Additional factors, clearly beyond people's control, include declining job opportunities, declining wages, declining public assistance, mental illness, and physical disability.

In some communities individual religious congregations have outreach programs for the poor and homeless. In the authors' community, the homeless are cared for by a private agency that is a partnership of forty-seven congregations. It runs a homeless shelter that provides short-term overnight sleeping space, with meals, showers, and a safe environment. Passes are issued daily from 6:00 a.m. to 4:30 p.m., with check-in between 9:00 p.m. and 10:00 p.m. The shelter closes at 7:00 a.m., after serving a light breakfast. Each night this shelter accommodates up to forty-six adults. Hundreds of volunteers manage the shelter and provide/serve the needs of the homeless.

Our state of Indiana, with nineteen shelters, is one of forty-six states on a homeless shelter list. Some of the states having the most shelters are

California with sixty-three, Michigan with fifty-two, Alabama with fifty-one, Georgia with thirty-two, and Texas with twenty-six.

Overall, lack of public housing is one of the main reasons for homelessness. The situation in post–Hurricane Katrina New Orleans is instructive. While one segment of the city has returned to normal, another segment, estimated conservatively to be 12,000 people, up from 6,000, lives on the streets. Some of the newly homeless are migrants from other states or even other countries. But many are native to New Orleans who returned to find marked declines in affordable housing and social services. By design, relatively little federal money for rebuilding was designated to rehabilitate affordable housing for renters, as opposed to going to homeowners. And despite a doubling of homelessness, the already inadequate shelter system dropped from 2,800 shelter beds to 2,045, some of which even charged a fee. Mental health and detox services are all but nonexistent for the homeless.[13]

As noted earlier, the United States lacks a national health care plan. The expense of private health insurance limits access to medical care for many, including those living in poverty and/or on the streets. In 2004, 16 percent of Americans had no health insurance, either private or employer-sponsored.[14] Moreover, 24 percent of the poor had no health insurance of any kind, despite the existence of government programs such as Medicaid and Medicare. Uninsured Americans are nearly four times less likely to see a doctor when they need one, and not seeing a doctor when necessary leads to illnesses and diseases that may cost taxpayers much more in the long run.

For those with some insurance, moreover, the coverage limits care, especially mental health care, by restricting the amount and type of services people can purchase. In addition, current procedures for screening people into care are particularly biased against racial and ethnic minorities who may not present or be judged to present standard symptoms.

THE ELDERLY

Unlike people in other age groups, in America there is ageism, or the systematic persecution and degradation of people who are old. Similar to sexism, racism, and heterosexism, with ageism the elderly are stereotyped as being less intelligent, less competent, and less active than younger people. They are often shunned, discriminated against in employment, and sometimes victims of abuse.

There is diversity among the elderly in terms of physical and social functioning. Thus, gerontologists, scientists who study aging and the aged, often divide the older population into three groups: those age 65–74, called the young-old; those age 75–84, called the middle-old; and those 85 and over, called the old-old or oldest old. Americans in these age groups are an increasingly large segment of the population with the old-old being the fastest growing segment of this population. From 1890 to 1920 the older population grew slowly, but from 1920 onward the rate of increase speeded up and by 2000 older Americans made up 12.6 percent of the entire population (34.8 million people). This growth is due to several factors: the retirement of the so-called "baby boomers" (those born between 1946 and 1964); the declining proportion of children in the population; and longer life expectancy.

The variability among older people is not only in terms of chronological age but also in terms of a number of other dimensions. Take gender, for example. Since women live longer than men, about five years on average, older women outnumber older men, especially from age seventy on. This results not only from biological differences but also from gender roles and lifestyles. For example, women are more likely than men to seek medical attention and to work in less dangerous jobs. There are some lifestyle changes among women that lessen the longevity of women, such as increased smoking, use of alcohol and other drugs, and stresses related to the "second shift" and caregiving for children and elderly family members. Nevertheless, as the elderly population itself grows older, older women are expected to increasingly outnumber older men. This gender difference in life expectancy is important because across all racial and ethnic groups, older women have fewer financial resources and are more likely to experience poverty than older men are.[15]

Marital status is another important dimension of variability among the elderly. Seventy-five percent of older men are married and have their spouses to rely on, whereas over half of older women are widowed. Women comprise most of the widowed because they tend to live longer than men, are usually three or four years younger than their husbands and thus more likely to outlive them, and widowers age sixty-five and older are eight times more likely than women to remarry.

Widowhood means that the elderly must deal with grief and mourning, feelings of sadness, longing, bewilderment, anguish, self-pity, anger, guilt, and loneliness, as well as relief. Almost half of elderly men and women are resilient and cope with the loss of their spouse with minimal grief, but about 16 percent experience chronic grief lasting more than eighteen months.[16]

Widows are likely to have two distinctive problems. One is financial, as the average living standard of widows drops 18 to 30 percent with the death of the husband. This is due importantly to loss of his Social Security income. Some widows are also ignorant about their family's finances, which they must learn to deal with. A second problem is loss of the role of wife, which may have been a central role. As noted above, widows have less chance of remarrying than do widowers.

As they get older the proportion of men whose wives have died increases, so that by age eighty-five, close to one-half of men are widowed. Widowers have their own problems, especially if there had been a traditional division of household labor between husband and wife. Such men are poorly prepared to take on the daily domestic matters of cooking, cleaning, and laundry. They have also lost their major source of intimacy and have to find sources other than the spouse for social support—advice, approval, caregiving.

Employment status also varies among the elderly. Prior to 1986, most workers were forced to retire at age sixty-five whether they wanted to or not. In single or traditional retirement, it is the husband who works and retires. As married women increasingly enter the labor force, however, they and their husbands are thereby affected. They adjust in one of three patterns: husband initially, wife initially, or synchronized in which the husband and wife retire at the same time. In general, incomes decline by one-third to one-half after retirement, and such a decrease pushes some elderly into poverty, especially the old-old.

In 1986, the U.S. Congress passed legislation ending mandatory retirement for most workers. Nevertheless, in 2000, the elderly were 3 percent of the labor force. This involved about 20 percent of men and 9 percent of women over age sixty-five. Why are these people working? There are several reasons, all related to finances.

First, in 1935 the Social Security Act was passed, now providing pension benefits to more than 90 percent of the elderly. However, the amount of benefits depends on the length of time people have been in the labor force and how much they have earned; in general, it replaces only 39 percent of an elderly person's preretirement income, forcing many to work. Second, in 2000 the Social Security Administration ended financial penalties for working past age sixty-five, so this was an incentive for older employees to continue working. Third, since the 1990s, many companies have reduced or eliminated their employee pension plans, causing many older people to continue working. Fourth, as indicated in chapter 4, there is less confidence among workers that they will have enough money to live comfortably after they retire, especially to pay for anticipated medical costs after retirement. This causes them to continue working.

The growth of the elderly population is important because many older people depend on their families, the government, or both for support in terms of finances, physical support, and emotional support. Many employers, on the other hand, complain about the costs of elder caregiving, while less than one-fourth of businesses offer employees elder care support services and benefits, such as flexible hours and telecommuting.

The government pension of Social Security has lifted many of the elderly out of poverty. For example, in 1959 about 35 percent of people over age sixty-five were poor, while in 2000 only about 10 percent of the elderly had incomes below the poverty line. The poverty rate for elderly minorities is between two and three times higher than for elderly whites. The poverty rate increases with age, and the number of Americans who will be eighty-five or older is expected to triple by 2030.

In general, older women are less well off financially than elderly men for several reasons, relating to their employment histories. Throughout their working years, they were more likely to work intermittently and receive lower earnings. Their segregation into lower-pay jobs also meant that they have smaller pensions, if any; less Social Security benefits; and smaller savings and assets.[17] If an older woman is married to a retired older man, she may receive a spousal "allotment" equal to one-half of her husband's benefit, or receive benefits calculated on her own employment record, which is often lower.

Despite low or moderate incomes, and having reared their children, a growing problem for seniors who are grandparents is that they are increasingly responsible for housing and rearing their grandchildren. This occurs because the parents will not or cannot care for their children, often because of emotional problems, alcohol abuse, or drug addiction. About 6 million grandparents, especially grandmothers, are caring for their grandchildren. This is about 6 percent of all children being reared this way. There is economic stress because nearly one-fourth of grandparents caring for grandchildren have incomes below the poverty line. There is also psychological stress for the elderly caregivers and a need for social support as they cope with their grandchildren's daily lives.

While grandparent caregiving cuts across gender, class, and race, it is twice as likely among African Americans.[18] Drug addiction of adult children is a leading cause. This leads grandparents to seeing their grown children's lives disintegrate and having to deal with the effects of prenatal drug use on the physical and mental health of the grandchildren for whom they are caring.

The living arrangements of older Americans vary by gender and race/ethnicity. Older women are less likely to live with their spouses (because husbands predecease them), and are more likely to live alone or with people other than their spouses. Among people aged sixty-five and older, African Americans, Asian Americans, and Hispanics are much more likely than whites to live with people other than their spouses; e.g., grown children, siblings, or other relatives.

As couples live longer together, the likelihood that one of them will get ill increases, and the healthy one, usually the wife, becomes caregiver to the other. If the elderly do not have a spouse to rely on, they usually turn to their children for help.

Between 70 and 80 percent of elderly adults have at least one living sibling and they can provide emotional and other help in times of need. Elderly siblings share a family history and provide potentially the longest lasting relationship in life. Relationships may have been close throughout life, or renewed in later life. Sister-sister relationships seem to be particularly important sources of social support.

In general, elderly people without either a spouse or adult children receive less personal care and have a higher rate of nursing-home residency than do older people with children. Overall, about 4.5 percent of elders live in nursing homes, most being women. The likelihood of living in a nursing home increases rapidly with age: 1 percent at age 65 to 74; 5 percent at age 75 to 84; and more than 18 percent at age 85 and over.[19] About 2 percent of elders live in homes for the aged and other group quarters. Less than 1 percent live in mental hospitals, tuberculosis hospitals, prisons, and institutions for the developmentally handicapped. Long-term care alternatives are increasingly necessary and are growing; they include in-home care, adult day care, assisted living apartments, small group homes, nursing facilities, and continuing care retirement communities. Cost, however, is an impediment for their use.

Who cares for elderly Americans when they can't take care of themselves? While elders are more likely than those in other age categories to engage in preventive health practices, their need for health care and personal care assistance is age-related. Health care needs include such things as catheter maintenance and injections, whereas personal care consists of help with daily activities such as bathing, doing housework, and preparing meals. The percent of elders who have severe needs for personal care, for example, increases from 5.4 percent at age 65 to 69 to 26.4 percent at age 95 and over.

Three-fourths of all long-term personal care services are provided by informal helpers, mostly spouses, adult children, and friends. Ideally most adult children in a given family would participate in parental caregiving in some way, but most elder care is provided by women, usually daughters or daughters-in-law.

Conflicts may arise involving previous unresolved antagonisms, the caregiver's inability to accept the elderly parent's increasing dependence, conflicts over loyalties between spousal or childrearing responsibilities and caring for the parent, and resentment, anger, and conflicts over money or inheritance matters. Elder caregiving seems to affect wives more negatively than husbands when they become a caregiver to a parent in the household. When caring for a parent out of the household, however, some women seem to gain a greater sense of self-esteem and purpose.

It is not only spouses and adult children who are providing care to elders. According to a National Alliance for Caregiving survey, about 1.4 million U.S. children aged eight to eighteen are caring for another family member, often a grandparent.[20] Thirty percent of child caregivers are aged twelve to fifteen. In general, someone else helps, also. But the care given by half of the children involves help with at least one activity of daily living, including bathing, dressing, or feeding. And almost all of the child caregivers help with such things as keeping the elder company, shopping, preparing meals, or doing other household tasks. In addition, young adult grandchildren are providing elder care as well. As is the case for adult caregivers, child caregivers need breaks, and support groups specifically designed for them. And when elders become incontinent or suffer from dementia, family and friends may get overwhelmed and need to turn to institutional options to ensure adequate care for the elder and to maintain the mental and physical health of the caregivers.

A growing concern among middle-aged lesbians and gays, especially those who do not have children or whose family has rejected them, is who will provide care when they get old. They fear that they will once again have to closet their sexual orientation when they enter retirement communities and nursing homes. There are some retirement communities, assisted-living facilities, and nursing homes marketed specifically to homosexuals, but many lesbians and gays will not be able to afford them.

It is estimated that from 1 percent to 10 percent of people over age sixty-five are abused or neglected. The most common form of elder maltreatment is neglect, such as failing to take them to receive necessary medical care or failing to provide adequate food, clean clothes, and a clean bed. Neglect is followed by physical abuse, which is inflicting injury or physical pain or sexual assault. Then there is psychological abuse, which includes verbal abuse, deprivation of mental health services, harassment, and deception. Social abuse involves unreasonable confinement and isolation, lack of supervision, and abandonment. And there is legal abuse, which is improper or illegal use of the elder's resources. One other type of elder abuse is called "granny dumping."[21] This is when adult children or grandchildren who feel burdened with the care of their elderly parent or grandparent drive the elder to a hospital and leave them at the entrance with no identification. The hospital is required by state law to take care of the elder or transfer the person to a nursing home, which is paid by state funds.

Such maltreatment results largely from caregiving stress and use of alcohol or other drugs. It is expected that such frustration will increase as baby boomers age, draining already limited resources for the elderly, forcing adult children and other family members to care for them with little government support. Stress can be lessened by giving the caregiver adequate forms of social support, links to community services, and training. Putting the responsibility on home care, however, will increasingly burden those doing the bulk of caregiving, women.

The United States has fragmented systems for financing health care and long-term personal care. They consist of Medicare, Medicaid, private health and long-term care insurance, and family savings. Medicare is a program of health insurance for older Americans that is administered by the Social Security Administration. It consists of two parts: hospital insurance, or Part A, and supplementary medical insurance, or Part B. Medicare is funded by three sources; namely, a payroll tax on the wages of working Americans, premiums paid by Medicare beneficiaries, and the general revenues of the United States. It has covered almost all Americans aged sixty-five or over since July 1, 1966, but coverage is not automatic. Older people must have participated in Social Security–covered employment or be the spouse, survivor, or former spouse of a covered worker.

Medicaid is a federal and state program to provide health care to the poor, regardless of their age, which is administered by local human services departments following federal guidelines and regulations. It is funded by federal and state revenues, and eligibility is based on economic status. Medicaid pays for everything that Medicare does, plus many other services such as long-term care in licensed nursing homes and home care in most states. Together Medicare and Medicaid provide over one-half of the funds used to provide health care to older people.

There are two types of private insurance policies that address elders' needs for paying for health and long-term care. One type is to supplement Medicare benefits, known as "Medigap" policies. In 2000, about 69 percent of elders covered by Medicare had such coverage. The policies primarily cover copayments and deductibles connected with services that Medicare covers. They are of no help in paying for long-term hospitalization and long-term care not covered by Medicare, leaving major gaps unfilled.

The second type of private insurance is long-term care policies, which have been written since 1982. Long-term care insurance has been slow to develop, bought primarily by middle-aged, middle-income people. Those aged above seventy do not buy long-term care insurance because the premiums are too high and/or they have the resources to self-insure. For people in their late forties or early fifties, however, premiums are low and do not increase with age, providing a slowing of the depletion of savings.

Our systems for financing health care for older Americans leave serious gaps. Medicare does not cover many aspects of care, and restrictive criteria keep Medicare support for long-term care very low. Medicaid covers many of the areas Medicare does not cover, but it is not available to most middle-class people. Private long-term care insurance is too expensive for those who wait until later life to buy it.

Similarly, there are difficulties in meeting personal care needs for many people. They are those who do not have sufficient income to pay for the needed help; those who not have family and friends who can help; those whose care needs are so serious that they require 24/7 supervision; and those for whom needed services are not available in the community or are not acceptable because the services are unreliable or of poor quality.

With the "graying" of society has come a right-to-die issue. Some elderly want to control their own death, rather than exist in pain or with loss of bodily functions and/or generally becoming increasingly helpless over time. In 1994 the voters of Oregon approved a referendum to legalize suicide assisted by a physician. The provisions of the proposal were that two different physicians had to agree that the patient was both terminally ill and mentally stable. Then the patient was to have the lethal prescription filled and to self-administer the drug. If the patient was not physically able to do this, s/he was not eligible for the "physician-aid-in-dying" process. After some attempts to appeal the referendum, the U.S. Supreme Court upheld Oregon's right-to-die law. In 1997, moreover, the Supreme Court left it up to the states to decide the legality of doctor-aided suicide.

In 1935, when the Social Security Act was passed, life expectancy was just below sixty-two years, compared to about seventy-eight today. The growth of the elderly population changes the relative size of working- and dependent-age groups. In 2000, for example, there was about one older person for every five working-age people, while by 2030 it is expected that there will be one older person being supported by fewer than three working-age people. Trends such as increases in rates of crime, substance abuse, out-of-wedlock births, and children living in poverty will result in a small group of people in the labor force supporting social service programs such as Social Security and health-care benefit for a large numbers of retirees. It is especially important to maintain Social Security, for unlike other groups, the elderly in America have seen a decline in poverty, from over 30 percent in 1959 to 10 percent in 2003. More than anything else, it is the social policy that created Social Security that has lifted many elderly Americans out of poverty.

The aging of the U.S. population calls for increased elder medical care as well as residential care. The growth of nursing homes and home care workers is the result. As noted earlier with respect to for-profit day care, the workers who provide the day-to-day care for the institutionalized elderly are usually women of color, many of them recent immigrants, and typically of limited training and income. And the same pressures to contain costs, meet government regulations, and conduct work in a bureaucratic manner mitigates against these caregivers providing social and emotional caregiving and against care recipients being able to preserve their dignity and autonomy.

Perhaps the greatest problem in providing adequate health and long-term care services to the elderly is the inflation in the health industry. In 1975 Medicare spent $517 per covered person; in 1980 it spent $1,142; in 1998 it spent $5,114; and the costs keep escalating. The challenge is to provide adequate and available health- and long-term care within the boundaries of what we as Americans are willing to pay.

THE INCARCERATED

Another group of marginalized and ignored Americans are those in jails and prisons. The United States incarcerates more people than any other country worldwide. The incarcerated now comprise 1 in 130 of the overall population, and 1 in 100 of the adult population. In terms of numbers of people, on December 31, 2006, there were 2,258,983 prisoners in federal or state prisons or in local jails. This was an increase of 2.9 percent from 2005. Federal or state jurisdiction accounted for 1,502,179 of them.

The number of women in state or federal prisons also increased from 2005, up 4.5 percent to 112,498 inmates. Among female offenders, there are more white women—93,500 or 94/100,000—but a higher rate of black women, 68,800 or 358/100,000, and Hispanic women, 32,400 or 152/100,000. The rate of increase in imprisonment exceeds overall changes in the crime rate and results largely from mandatory sentencing policies.

At year end 2006, there were 3,042 black males sentenced to prisons per 100,000 black males in the population, compared to 1,261 Hispanic males and 487 white males. Looked at another way, 12.6 percent of black males age 20 to 34 are in prison, compared to 3.6 percent of Hispanic males and 1.7 percent of white males. These rates are on a given day. Over many years, the rates will be much higher. The Bureau of Justice statistics say that 28 percent of black men will be sent to jail or prison in their lifetime.[22]

The United States started a so-called "war on drugs" in 1969 under President Nixon, and it continued full force through the terms of Presidents Reagan and Clinton. While whites, who are the majority of the overall population, constitute most of those arrested on drug-related charges, African Americans are arrested at three times the rate of their representation in the population.

Felony drug offenders, unlike almost every other category of offender, stand to lose the opportunity to receive public assistance (Temporary Assistance for Needy Families or TANF), food assistance, higher education funding, and income tax deductions for pursuing a college degree.

In 2004, state prisons had 633,700 prisoners serving time for violent offenses (52 percent), 265,000 for property offenses (21 percent), and 249,400 for drug offenses (26 percent).[23] Another 7 percent were in prison for public-order offenses. While imprisonment may cut crime and be appropriate for serious offenders such as murderers and rapists, it may not be for nonviolent offenders, such as those arrested for driving drunk (DWI).

The cost is increasingly a large part of states' budgets—an average of nearly $24,000 per prisoner per year. This cost is causing some states to make major changes with respect to nonviolent offenders. Texas, for example, expanded drug programs and drug courts and revised parole practices.

According to a federal Household Survey, the overwhelming majority of drug users are white (9.9 million or 72 percent), compared to 2.2 million blacks (15 percent) and 1.4 million Hispanics (10 percent). However, of the state prison inmates serving time for drug offenses at year end 2004, 112,500 or 45.1 percent were black, compared to 51,000 or 20.8 percent who were Hispanic and 65,500 or 26.4 percent who were white.[24]

One of the more despicable features of a punitive prison system is the impediments created to helping prisoners stay connected with family members. One would think that telephone calls from prisoners to their children, spouses, or other family members would be encouraged, because of their role in rehabilitation of inmates. Unfortunately, in the prison system the opposite seems to be the case. Henry Fernandez is the spouse of a public defender in Pennsylvania, and he noticed that the collect calls from prisoners about defense work were being billed at very high costs. Prisoners usually cannot receive telephone calls and must make collect calls to family or attorneys using the telephone service contracted by the prison. What do families of prisoners pay to accept collect calls from a son or daughter, or a mother or father?

Fernandez reports that collect calls from prisoners to their homes were billed at about $1.07 per minute.[25] If a prisoner called home once a week for fifteen minutes to stay connected with children or parents, the families receiving the collect calls would pay a total of $834.00 per year. But Fernandez found that residents of Pennsylvania could have unlimited calling anywhere in the United States for about $480.00 per year. So why wouldn't a prison renegotiate with telephone service providers to obtain the lowest possible rate for collect calls from the prison? Given the fact that contact with families contributes to prisoner rehabilitation, one would think that the telephone calling to parents, spouses, and children would be encouraged. Instead, the families of prisoners, who tend to be in the low-income bracket, are overcharged for telephone services. As Fernandez states:

> States ought to stop the pathetic practice of gouging poor families who just want to keep in touch with loved ones in prison. It's mean-spirited and bad policy. It should end.

Prison living conditions are harsh, regimented, and degrading for both men and women inmates.[26] Women have more rules imposed on them and are punished more harshly than men for rule infractions. Educational and vocational programming is less available in women's prisons, and that which exists does not prepare women to survive economically or provide adequately for their families upon release (e.g., clerical work, cosmetology, and garment manufacturing). Programming in men's prisons focuses on the skilled trades; that is, carpentry, electronics, plumbing, and construction.

Moreover, in 1994 Congress eliminated prisoner's eligibility for Pell Grants for college attendance. Lack of such educational assistance is particularly ironic in that prisoner participation in GED programs, and especially postsecondary education, has been shown to reduce recidivism and help in getting employment after release.

Relatively few prisons offer programs to address problems associated with physical and sexual abuse, in spite of almost one-half of women inmates reporting having been previously physically or sexually abused. Moreover, most women inmates are guarded by men, some of whom sexually exploit women prisoners.

Separation from their children limits women's caretaking ability, despite the fact that about two-thirds of female inmates have children less than eighteen years old who had been living with them. Only about one-quarter live with the father. The remainder of these children live with a grandparent, or other relative, or are placed in foster homes or institutional care. Prisons vary widely in the amount of time mothers are allowed to visit with their children, either in the prison or on furloughs at home or in halfway houses. Most visits, moreover, are by mail or on the telephone because most prisons are located more than one hundred miles from inmates' homes. Separation of mothers and children has serious psychological consequences for both parties.

Each year, an estimated 600,000 inmates are released and returned to the community. More than one-half of those released will be reincarcerated within three years of release. This revolving door of release and reimprisonment is costly in both human and financial terms and demands a massive effort to try to change this destructive pattern. The 600,000 inmates reentering the community each year join the approximately 12 million in the community who have prior felony convictions. Finding steady work for ex-offenders is the key to reducing incentives for crime and reducing recidivism.[27] After serving time in prison, ex-offenders face major challenges in finding jobs, housing, and general assistance to deal with reintegrating into the community. This requires prisons to provide educational programs, job training programs, and rehabilitation programs dealing with anger management, alcohol use, and drug use. Programs within prisons need to be linked with postrelease programs to provide continuity of services and a consistent message that there is a second chance for those who want to work at it. National public opinion polls indicate that the U.S. public gives their overwhelming support for rehabilitative services as opposed to a punishment-only system.[28] And with almost unanimous bipartisan support, the U.S. Congress has passed the Second Chance Act, which is to provide money and leadership in making rehabilitation a central goal of the federal justice system.

In sum, the United States has a dire need for caring services for the poor, homeless, aged, and incarcerated. This is a major public challenge and responsibility given that these four groups of Americans number at least 35 million.

8

Confronting the Crisis

At this point in the book our argument should be clear: starting in the mid-1970s and continuing today, the American economic and political systems have changed in ways that have reduced the options for hope, trust, and caring for most Americans. As noted especially in chapter 2, the country has been undergoing a long process of deindustrialization and job relocation by industries aiming to increase profits by moving or starting their operations in low-wage, nonunion states and low-wage countries around the world. This has been accompanied by increasing joblessness and an increasing income gap for the most prosperous top 20 percent of Americans versus the bottom 80 percent of working Americans who are increasingly insecure about their jobs. These trends have (1) resulted in 35 million Americans living below the poverty line, (2) been accompanied by a decline in affordable housing, (3) put increasing pressure on dual-earner families to meet their family and financial responsibilities, and (4) deflected attention and support for older Americans and those in nursing homes and prisons.[1]

Most of the solutions that have been offered to these problems focus on the problems of the displaced workers rather than changing the policies that have produced the displaced workers. Consider, for example, the views of Paul Krugman, a liberal economist and Nobel Laureate who can be considered a friend of workers and a harsh critic of corporate America. Krugman has taken the position that the growing trade between high-wage and low-wage countries is a good thing for this country, but that "for American workers the story is much less positive. In fact it's hard to avoid the conclusion that growing U.S. trade with third world countries reduces the real wages of many and perhaps most workers in this country."[2] After acknowledging that the import of manufactured goods has almost tripled between 1990 and 2006, he states: "So am I arguing for protectionism? No . . . keeping world markets relatively open is crucial to the hopes of billions of people . . . For the sake of the world as a whole, I hope that we respond to the trouble with trade not by shutting trade down, but by doing things like strengthening the social safety net."

Krugman's views are consistent with the editors of the *New York Times*, where Krugman's columns appear. The *Times* acknowledges that trade disrupts life, but it is concerned that presidential candidates Barack Obama and Hillary Clinton, in their primary battle, were critical of NAFTA and called for renegotiating the terms of the agreement. The *Times* acknowledges growing income inequality but claims that this has little to do with trade; rather it is because of a shortage of education and skilled workers and a slowdown in high school and college graduation rates. The *Times* solution: "expanding the social safety net to help workers displaced by trade."[3]

Of course, it is important to provide a safety net for the workers and their families, such as unemployment insurance, wage insurance, and funds for retraining and education. But retraining is only meaningful if there are jobs for retrained workers. If we do nothing more than strengthen the social safety net by making it more generous, we are really writing off that generation of displaced workers and saying that they must be sacrificed for the good of the whole world.

Can we provide realistic remedies to this crisis of hope, trust, and caring? The objective of this chapter is to present remedies for your consideration. The remedies we present for consideration require resources for their implementation, and these resources are investment capital, political capital, and social capital. Investment capital means money, and some of our proposed remedies will require substantial investment of the public's money. Where will this money come from? There are only two possible places: new taxes on individual and corporate income and reassigned money from one budget line to another. There are only three large pools of money in the current federal budget that are available for reassignment: Social Security, Medicare/Medicaid, and the defense budget. The first two money pools are entitlements that are not likely to be targeted for reallocation; that leaves the defense budget as the main source for new money.

Political capital means that elected officials have the will and the motivation to mobilize the support of their colleagues and the public for new initiatives. New projects requiring major new spending must be presented to the American people with clarity and honesty. The government should organize public meetings across the country to inform and involve the public about why a new project is needed and how it will work to make things better for most Americans. The consequences of inadequate efforts to have public discussion of important issues can be seen in the public reaction to the early efforts by the president and Congress to restore credit and confidence in our financial system in 2008. The American public initially believed that they were being rushed into solving a problem that was not of their making and without their full participation, and they expressed overwhelming disapproval of the plan to spend $700 billion of taxpayer money to restore confidence in the financial system. There was a very good argument for this "bailout," but the rush to pass the bill left most Americans in the dark about why the plan was needed, what were the alternatives, and how would the various plans work. In hindsight, the early handling of the 2008 financial crisis was clearly not the way to ask the American public to support a new project.

Finally, social capital means the people-to-people connections that can grow exponentially and become the power for mobilizing citizen support for our proposed remedies. If there is to be genuine public support for a project, the public must be informed fully and honestly about the possible pain and gain of a new proposal. Moreover, they must be given the time to discuss matters with their friends and neighbors, with their elected officials, and have the opportunity to provide their views on the proposed project. If done properly, new public projects, of the sort that we will present in this chapter, can generate the trust and support of the people (i.e., social capital) to make the project a success.

As we think about how to restore hope, trust, and caring into American life, it is important to distinguish between "top down" solutions by government and "bottom up" solutions that require voluntary actions from most, if not all, Americans. Solutions based on government actions often serve to divide Americans because people often think about "who is paying" for a new program and "who is receiving benefits" from the program. Moreover, the American people are well aware that since government programs involve spending the taxpayer's money, they have a right to ask the cost-benefit question, even though it may be divisive. In contrast, voluntary actions to solve societal problems require Americans to become partners in a solution and to demonstrate how everyone has something to gain from a new program. This means that although it is possible to develop programs that can restore hope to Americans, such as creating greater job security, the programs can be perceived as unfair if the costs or benefits are not shared by all. If a proposed solution is not believed to be fair, it will lead to an erosion of trust and a failure to restore hope. The ideal solution to a societal problem is one that can restore both hope and trust because the majority of Americans believe that it is good for the country and for them.

We believe that the American people today are eager for new ideas that will improve their lives and restore a sense of security for their future. We believe this for two reasons. First, we sense the growth of a movement for economic populism, reflected in the growing disconnect between national policies on trade and taxation and job security of the American worker. Americans have become increasingly aware of the connection between massive job losses and declining wages on the one hand and national trade policies like NAFTA on the other hand. NAFTA was sold to the American people as the best way to expand trade and expand jobs and wages for American workers. The average American family knows that the effect of NAFTA is the opposite of what was promised, and they are not going to be fooled a second time. One observer of this development has called this economic populism a resurgent nationalism, which is neither totally conservative nor totally liberal.[4] Both the political left and the political right support this new nationalism-populism, with the liberals criticizing global economic policies and the conservatives attacking illegal immigrants who take jobs from Americans and depress wages. If members of Congress who are willing to break with their party and abandon the old orthodoxies can harness this wave of economic populism, then we have the potential to focus on job creation, wages, and job security. It is this new focus that would, in our view, restore hope to the American people.

The second reason for our optimism is that we think that the time is ripe for the earthly equivalent of President John F. Kennedy's May 25, 1961, call to Americans that it is "time for a great new American enterprise." He asked Americans to join with him in a pledge to put a man on the moon by the end of the decade. He asked Americans to join in the heavy burden of this new project (spending tax dollars) and he linked it to our cold war struggle with the Soviet Union (which had already beaten the United States into space). And what would this great new earthly enterprise be? We think that it can be the rebuilding of America's deteriorating infrastructure. Almost daily, Americans are told about the congestion of the interstate highways and the deterioration of their state roads; about the number of structurally deficient and obsolete bridges; about the inability to clean up toxic waste sites; about the deteriorating public parks, beaches, and recreational harbors across the nation; about the absence of a modern transit infrastructure; and about the declining condition of America's schools. The list goes on and on, and the frailty of our infrastructure is dramatized by high-profile disasters such as the failure of the levees to protect New Orleans from Katrina and the collapse of a major bridge in Minneapolis.

The American Society of Civil Engineers published an Infrastructure Report Card in 2005, in which they assessed the conditions of public infrastructure in fifteen areas and assigned a grade to each (A=Exceptional, B=Good, C=Mediocre, D=Poor, F= Failure, I=Incomplete).[5] Here are the grades assigned by the ASCE in the fifteen areas.

Aviation	D+
Bridges	C
Dams	D
Drinking Water	D-
Energy (National Power Grid)	D
Hazardous Waste	D
Navigable Waterways	D-
Public Parks	C-
Rail	C-
Roads	D
Schools	D
Security	I
Solid Waste	C+
Transit	D+
Wastewater	D-

The report is not good, and all Americans would be potential beneficiaries from bringing our aging and deteriorating public infrastructure into the twenty-first century. This is the time for another "moon mission," but this time we should land in the United States.

As we present remedies designed to restore hope, trust, and caring, we will try to identify the resources that will be needed for their acceptance and implementation. Our general philosophy when proposing remedies is to make it as feasible as possible to have many different groups involved in sharing the pain and sharing the gain of any proposed remedy. That means that the costs in terms of public money (taxes) and private money (individual and business contributions) have to be widely shared. The problem with many solutions offered by politicians today is that people often feel that the government is spending their money to provide help to people who are only a little worse off than they are. As we stated in chapter 1, the deficiencies of hope, trust, and caring are interrelated. People without hope are not likely to trust their government, and they are not likely to have the emotional resources to be very caring of others who may be less fortunate.

The remedies that we propose will involve political struggle because there are entrenched interests in the status quo. For example, there are a great many beneficiaries of a robust defense budget including big defense contractors, universities, engineers and scientists, and skilled blue-collar defense industry workers. An entrenched privileged class can be expected to defend their interests and to oppose efforts to increase taxes on corporations and on individual incomes on the top 1 to 5 percent of wealthiest Americans.

Ideally, we hope to propose solutions that can mobilize widespread support among Americans because they will recognize that all will benefit. We believe that the proposal that we offer to rebuild America's infrastructure can be such a proposal. However, some proposals may require the entrenched privileged class to accept higher taxes or to support more spending on social programs for Americans who have been left behind (chapter 7). The privileged class will argue that such programs will discourage investment and will ultimately be bad for the economy, and they will mobilize all their allies in the political, economic, and cultural sectors. In such cases, we must be prepared for political struggle between groups with opposed interests. The privileged class dominates the American political system through their control of the media, policy-making organizations, lobbying groups, political action organizations, and elite universities. This power network is formidable and can be expected to try to defeat any change in the "way we do business." But there is an alternative power network composed of public interest groups, progressive policy groups, alternative media, and some progressive political leaders.[6] We believe that this network can be mobilized to work together to build public support for the kind of reforms we propose.

RESTORING HOPE

Hope is about people feeling confident that they will have a job today and in the future. This kind of confidence gives people a greater sense of control over their lives, making them willing to do things today that will continue in the future. For example, they will be willing to plan for the future of their children, such as saving for their college education. They will also be willing to start a business or buy a home, because they are confident they can be successful with these risk-taking projects. The key to restoring hope requires a combination of creating jobs and making existing jobs more secure. We propose a two-pronged national project to restore jobs to American workers.

Create New Jobs

The first effort is to establish a project we call Jobs for America, and it would be based on the voluntary contributions of citizens along with matching contributions from federal and state governments and national labor unions. We believe that this project should have the highest priority because it would create secure jobs, which is the best way to restore hope, and it would build trust because of citizen involvement. The project should be developed as a high-profile national movement headed by a highly regarded public figure, with a board of advisers capable of mobilizing support for the project. The first stage of the project calls for a national plan to rebuild America's infrastructure of roads, bridges, highways, public buildings, and parks. In a second stage, the project would provide new support personnel for America's schools, libraries, hospitals, nursing homes, and prisons. This would employ millions of Americans in the years ahead, and it would be expensive, because such public-sector jobs would require enhanced pay and benefits. But we believe that it could be funded without requiring new taxes, which is very important. Most Americans are in a "no new taxes" way of thinking. We believe that the reason for this is that they don't trust their elected officials to use their money in ways that benefit the average American. We further believe that Americans are a generous people and they would help to fund an effort that benefits all Americans. Where would the money come from? How would the project work?

- When Americans file their tax returns each April 15, they would be invited to make a voluntary contribution to the Jobs for America project. They could contribute between $100 and $500 to the project by adding their contribution to the tax they owe, or deduct their contribution from the rebate that they are due. A taxpayer who owes $800 in taxes could contribute $200 to Jobs for Americans and thereby owe the IRS $1,000. Similarly, if a taxpayer is due for a $200 return, s/he could donate that amount to Jobs for America and not take a return. If 20 million taxpayers contributed an average of $100 to Jobs for America when they filed their taxes, this would provide $2 billion. In 2006, over 132 million Americans filed income tax returns. Of these, 43.4 million had zero or negative tax liability, leaving a pool of over almost 90 million taxpayers from which to get 20 million Americans to contribute to the Jobs for America project.
- Congress would become a partner with the citizens' voluntary contributions by making their own contribution at tax time and by enacting legislation that would provide a match, let's say five to ten times what taxpayers contribute; in this example, $10 to $20 billion. Where would the matching money come from? Congress would shift the money from the $519 billion defense budget, which is robust enough to be able to accommodate such an annual reallocation. The 2009 defense budget allocates $129 billion for personnel, $180 billion for maintenance activities, $80 billion for research and development, $24 billion for construction, $2 billion for management, and finally, $104 billion for procurement. We propose that the Jobs for America money should be shifted from the procurement budget, which is for the purchase of new fighter planes and weapons systems, and is usually a very padded budget. This practice would have the further advantage of gradually shifting funds from wartime spending to peacetime spending.
- Another potential source of funds for reallocation is the National Aeronautics and Space Agency. Since the beginning of the space program

in 1958, NASA's annual budget has been an average of $16 billion, or $810 billion over the past fifty years. We could delay further space exploration in favor of greater Earth exploration and use NASA money and defense money to fund Jobs for America.

- Infrastructure rebuilding projects would be located in each state, so when state governments applied for infrastructure rebuilding funds they would have to make a matching contribution, either financial or in-kind.
- National labor unions would provide some of the skilled carpenters, electricians, and masons who would be at the heart of the rebuilding projects. They would be expected to make a buy-in contribution to give them a partner status. Many unions lack the funds to make large-dollar contributions, but they could make some wage and work rules concessions that would help reduce the cost of the rebuilding projects.

We believe that this is the kind of project that Americans would support. It would cost all the partners something, but the gains would also benefit everyone in the form of job creation, economic stimulus, and new infrastructure in states and communities across the country. The key to this project would be getting the support of Americans to become voluntary contributors, and there would need to be a national public education effort about the Jobs for America project. The help of national advertising firms would be needed to develop the public education message, and the national media would be needed to deliver the message to America. All Americans would have to buy into the Jobs for America project if it is to have a chance for working, because this would be more than a one-time commitment. It may take five to ten years of putting billions of dollars into rebuilding America's infrastructure. The costs are high, but the benefits to working Americans are higher, and the benefits to the goal of restoring hope are enormous.

If the Jobs for America project is successful in getting support from the American people, it could be gradually shifted from voluntary annual contributions of American taxpayers to a fully funded national public infrastructure project. Of course, this would mean using public tax dollars, but we believe the public would support such an effort because of the widespread benefits of rebuilding infrastructure in every state with American workers.

Compare this jobs-centered approach with the bipartisan congressional stimulus package passed in early 2008. Congress and the president developed legislation to give Americans $150 billion in tax refunds in order to stimulate a slowing economy and to avoid recession. Putting this much new money into the hands of Americans is designed to stimulate aggregate demand for goods and services and thereby stimulate a sluggish economy.

What is less certain is whether this stimulus package will create jobs. Why? Because some Americans will use their stimulus checks to pay down existing debt; others may buy consumer goods that are likely to be imported from other countries; and some will just "squirrel it away" for a rainier day. In our view, the $150 billion would be better spent on our Jobs for America project because it would guarantee both job creation and infrastructure improvement, both of which would benefit most Americans.

Given the impact of the 2008 Wall Street crisis and recession on American jobs, an alternative to this grassroots Jobs for America program would be a fully funded version of this proposal, requiring Congress and the president to allocate at least $300 billion to begin rebuilding the crumbling infrastructure across the United States.

Save Jobs

What is needed to save existing jobs is to have a national industrial policy that identifies critical sectors of the economy for support in times of economic difficulty. While it is too late now for some sectors, this would have meant helping the steel industry, auto industry, and textile industry in the 1970s and 1980s when they were facing competition from firms in other countries. Instead of protecting U.S. industry, our government had policies that encouraged firms to ship their jobs and investment abroad. The Japanese had an industrial policy in the 1980s that helped their auto industry become competitive in the global auto industry. Such a policy would now seek a balance between trade and protecting U.S. industries. Critical sectors are those with the largest number of employees and with the greatest secondary effects on other sectors.

Current U.S. trade deficits involve importing to America consumer goods that were once produced by U.S. companies. Foreign trade statistics for 2007 identify "the principal end-use commodity categories" of imported goods. While the large dollar amount of end-use imports involved petroleum and natural gas ($635 million), the other imports include computers, electrical apparatus, and medicinal equipment ($444 million), and consumer goods like clothing, household goods, toys, TVs, and sporting goods ($475 million).[7] Surely, with a projobs industrial policy to create jobs in vital sectors, many of the now-imported goods could be produced in the United States by American workers.

- What the government can do now is to develop policies that both discourage companies from cutting jobs in the United States and sending them to other countries and rewarding companies that expand employment in their U.S. firms. We already have a model for how this is done. When the U.S. auto firms like General Motors and Ford decided that they must cut their workforce in order to survive in the competitive auto market, they offered workers buyouts averaging about $40,000. They also provided options to allow workers to receive $15,000 a year for four years of tuition and a stipend amounting to 50 percent of their wage. Using this experience as a model, we could require companies that decide to cut their workforce and expand production abroad to pay a tax that the government would use as part of a safety net and re-training/education program. The tax should be based on the difference between the wage paid to their laid-off domestic workers and the wage paid to foreign workers. On the other side of the ledger, when companies expand their workforce and when new companies are created, they should receive tax breaks that would contribute to their chances to be successful.

- Congress should pass legislation to prevent companies that have engaged in large-scale layoffs of domestic workers from making requests for H-1B visas to import foreign workers. Such requests for visas for foreign workers should be denied if the company has engaged in massive layoffs of domestic workers.
- Congress should review all government subsidies and federal contracts to firms that engage in massive layoffs of domestic workers at the same time they are increasing their foreign workforce.

Expand Opportunity

Restoring hope depends on the availability of secure jobs for Americans, but it also requires that each new generation of children has an equal chance of making the most of their abilities. What this means is that students in elementary schools and high schools should have access to the best teachers, curricula, and facilities and thereby have the best education that can be offered. The problem with this idealized goal is that the quality of education requires comparable resources to provide that quality, whereas there are big differences between resource-rich schools in the suburbs compared with resource-poor schools in the inner city and in rural areas. Unless there is comparability in the quality of school programs, students in the lesser-quality programs will not be afforded the same opportunity to compete in the labor market or in the education market. What can be done to provide all students with a comparable educational experience?

- Federal and state governments along with their departments of education must devise a national plan to provide comparable per-pupil expenditures for all schools. At present (2006), wealthy suburban schools spend nearly twice as much per pupil as inner city schools, and they can thereby hire the best teachers, provide smaller classes, and provide better facilities.[8] Equalizing resources could result in closing the achievement gap between students from the privileged class and those from moderate- and low-income areas and thereby increase the motivation for going to college.

- As noted in chapter 5, affirmative action programs to improve admission and funding for students who have traditionally been excluded from higher education should be modified to include economic criteria as well as race, gender, or ethnicity. This would mean that students of any color, ethnicity, or gender from families with limited income would be eligible for preferential admission and financial support to attend college.

- Break the pattern of residential segregation by providing a new public low-income rental-housing program to locate low-income children near good schools and their parents near entry-level jobs. Additionally, there should be an expansion of vouchers to families already living in public housing for their use to rent affordable apartments in other neighborhoods.

RESTORING TRUST

Restoring the American people's confidence in their social institutions, especially government and political leaders, will require, first and foremost, a plan to get money out of politics. This means reducing the dependence of politicians on contributions from wealthy donors, corporations, lobbyists, political action committees, interest groups, and labor unions. It will also require a dramatic change in business as usual, meaning we must change tax laws that provide rich Americans and corporations with numerous ways to delay, defer, and avoid taxes. We must also eliminate the dozens of "sweet deals" given to multinational corporations that encourage them to invest abroad and to avoid paying their fair share of taxes.[9] What can be done?

- The best way to get money out of politics is to enact a term limits law limiting representatives to three two-year terms, and senators to two four-year terms. With limited terms, members of Congress would no longer spend most of their time raising money in order to get ready for the next election. Mandated turnover in elected officials would weaken the lobbyist-politician link because the politician would not be around long enough to continue to provide favors. It would also get rid of the "safe seat" Congress members who get reelected numerous times, allowing them to become chairs of powerful committees, thereby providing even more favors to big donors. There is widespread public support for term limits as reported by national poll data and by the results of term limits referenda in twenty-three states in the 1990s; all were approved by very large margins.

Term limits for Congress would restore the ideal of a "citizen politician," the persons who leave a primary occupation to serve the country for a brief time and returns to their community to resume their prior life. Compare this ideal of diverse citizen participation to the 109th Congress, which had 228 attorneys (43 percent), 275 former state legislators (51 percent), 109 former congressional staffers, 35 former mayors, and 19 state governors or lieutenant governors. This concentration of career politicians who would, if they could, probably remain in Congress for life, overwhelms the handful of medical doctors (13), ministers (6), physical scientists (7), Peace Corp volunteers (6), and former FBI/CIA agents (3). In short, the 109th Congress hardly looks like a collection of citizen politicians, but a term limits law could change these patterns.

However, despite our belief in the merits of term limits, there is a valid opposing argument that views long-term tenure in Congress as producing more knowledgeable and effective representatives who are better able to serve constituents.

- Trust must also be restored among the identity politics groups that are in competition for public support of their various agendas. In chapter 5, we presented an affirmative action plan that included economic criteria for college admission and funding that would allow members of all identity groups to benefit. No one would be excluded on the basis of race, ethnicity, or gender; rather, exclusions would be on the basis of family income. We would encourage identity groups to find other ways to work together to advance common interests, rather than pursuing programs that advance the members of one group at the expense of members of another group.

RESTORE CARING

Caring is expressed in personal relationships with people who are important to you, such as immediate family, other kin, and close friends. This kind of caring is about providing help and support for people who are important to you, and it sometimes means putting their welfare on equal par with your own well being. But in order to provide this kind of caring, the caregiver has to have the resources to do so, namely the financial means, the time, and the emotional capacity. In short, it takes a healthy caregiver to be a dependable source of help to others. We will offer some examples of how public policies of governments and employers can help caregivers and make them effective in their interpersonal relationships with people who depend on them.

A second meaning of caring is being concerned about the well being of people whom you don't know. These are people who are members of marginalized and stigmatized groups. They are often people for whom it is difficult to express caring, for they are often responsible in part for their own problems; they are sometimes their own worst enemies. Expressing care for marginalized and stigmatized people like the poor, the aged, and the imprisoned takes the form of supporting public initiatives to help these less-fortunate Americans. People will be able to support these public initiatives only when they feel that they themselves are not living in conditions of financial or emotional need. That is part of the interconnected cycle of hope, trust, and caring. People will not express concern and caring for the less fortunate until those who are called upon to be care-policy supporters are themselves secure with their feelings of hope and trust.

- Parents are caregivers for their children and for other members of their family, most often their aging parents. Caregiving requires time, and in some cases money, to be able to help others. Caregivers who are not in the labor force, most likely mothers, are not covered by Social Security, unemployment, or workman's compensation. Their work patterns adapt to their caregiving responsibilities, making them economically vulnerable. Social Security regulations should be changed to recognize nonstandard work patterns and to take into account unpaid home-based work.
- Parents who are in the labor force need to have paid personal days provided by their employer to care for sick children or an aging parent. If an employer cannot afford the cost of paid family-care days, they could consider creating a voluntary pool of family day credits. For example, if one employee gets paid time off for four hours, another employee could volunteer to cover for that lost work and thereby earn four hours of family-time credit to be used when needed.
- Affordable child care should be provided by government and employers by providing a subsidy that will cover a percentage of the employees' cost. Some companies already provide on-site child care, which is the most desirable option, but this may not be feasible for many companies.
- "Human capital" should be promoted by improving the education, marketable skills, and self-discipline of school-age children. There should be mandatory early childhood education programs for low-income families.
- All states should create partnerships between public universities and resource-poor schools in their area to develop programs to enhance

the educational experience, reduce dropout rates, and provide students with better preparation for college. Some of the resources of public universities should be directed to assist elementary and secondary schools in low-income areas.

- America's most successful poverty reduction program, the Earned Income Tax Credit (EITC), should be expanded in terms of the credits and to make childless workers eligible. At present, this program provides a refundable tax credit to single parents and couples as a supplement to their income for each qualifying child. A family receives a supplement of $2,853 for one child and $ 4,716 for two or more qualifying children. The supplement is phased out when family income increases beyond $15,399.
- Federal and state funds should be directed to in-home care, including assistance with daily living activities to needy elderly. States should use their community college system to develop new programs for training licensed elder-care providers who would play a key role in keeping elder Americans at home.
- Medicare should be expanded to cover services now covered by Medicaid. While this falls short of proposals for universal health care, it increases services until the former could be achieved.
- Public education campaigns should be developed about long-term care insurance and should be directed to middle-aged persons so that they can take out policies while they are affordable. The looming crisis about paying for long-term care should be placed on the public agenda to develop policies to assist elderly Americans.
- Sentencing guidelines for drug convictions should be reexamined with the goal of reducing incarceration for nonviolent offenders. Such offenders should be offered probation involving job training and work opportunities that will get their lives moving in a positive direction. The goal is to reduce the incarceration rates of young men and women charged with nonviolent drug convictions.
- Congress should expand funding for two pieces of legislation designed to assist released prisoners, the Prisoner Reentry Initiative of 2004 and the Second Chance Act of 2008. Both acts provide mentoring and transitional services for persons reentering the community. Federal funds should be provided to federal and state prisons to enable them to select prisoners scheduled for reentry into the community, remove them from the prison environment, and place them in a special facility for intensive transitional services related to substance abuse, anger management, job training, job placement, and housing.

Although America is the richest and most powerful nation in the world, nothing lasts forever, and for the last thirty years or so America has gone down a path that threatens its continued viability as the place where most people want to live and raise their children. We believe that the triple crises of hope, trust, and caring threaten to make America a very different country, one different in ways that only the privileged class of Americans will not recognize or understand. The privileged class will continue to enjoy high levels of income, wealth, and security, and their gated-community lives will protect them somewhat from seeing how the other 80 percent are living. But this kind of polarized society is not sustainable. Eventually those who are continuously excluded from the American Dream will submit a bill for payment of their real grievances.

We believe that the intersection of the presidential election and the economic crisis has provided President Obama with the political opportunity to consider the type of proposals that we have presented and to take America in a new direction. The actions of the new administration will determine whether America remains at the crossroads or embarks on a new path to meet the needs of most of its citizens.

Notes

CHAPTER 1

1. "Let's Take This Country Back," *Washington Spectator* (New York: Public Concern Foundation, 2006).

2. Robert Perrucci and Shelley MacDermid, "Time and Control in a 24/7 Environment: Clock Time, Work Time, Family Time," in *Workplace Temporalities: Research in the Sociology of Work*, ed. Beth Rubin (New York: JAI Press), 343–68.

3. Jill Andresky Fraser, *White Collar Sweatshop: The Deterioration of Work and Its Rewards in Corporate America* (New York: W. W. Norton, 2001).

4. Barry Bluestone and Bennett Harrison, *The Deindustrialization of America* (New York: Basic Books, 1982).

5. Arne Kalleberg, "Flexible Firms and Labor Market Segmentation: Effects of Workplace Restructuring on Jobs and Workers," *Work and Occupations* (May 2003): 154–75.

6. Robert Perrucci and Cynthia Stohl, "Economic Restructuring and Changing Corporate-Worker-Community Relations: Searching for a New Social Contract," in *Research in the Sociology of Work*, volume 6, ed. Randy Hodson (Greenwich, CT: JAI Press, 1997), 177–95.

7. Dan Clawson, *The Next Upsurge: Labor and New Social Movements* (Ithaca, NY: Cornell University Press, 2003).

8. Economic Policy Institute, "Family Income Limits by Quintile, 1974–2004: Share of Aggregate Family Income by Quintile." Available at http://www.epinet.org.

9. David Wright, "Changes in Hourly Earnings and Weekly Earnings, 1947–2005," *Work Series*, Wichita State University, November 2006, A19–A20.

CHAPTER 2

1. Brink Lindsey, "Job Losses and Trade: A Reality Check," Trade Briefing Paper 19, Cato Institute, March 17, 2004.

2. Gallup Poll, "Americans' Economic Pessimism Reaches Record High." Reported in Paul Krugman, "Winter of Our Discontent," *New York Times* (November 26, 2007); David Leonhardt and Marjorie Connelly, "81% in Poll Say Nation Is Headed on Wrong Track," *New York Times* (April 4, 2008).

3. Lawrence Mishel, Jared Bernstein, and Sylvia Allegretto, *The State of Working America, 2004/2005* (Ithaca, NY: Cornell University Press, 2005).

4. Mike Davis, *Prisoners of the American Dream: Politics and Economy in the History of the U.S. Working Class* (London: Verso, 1986).

5. Robert B. Reich, *The Next American Frontier* (New York: Time Books, 1983).

6. Carolyn C. Perrucci, Robert Perrucci, Dena B. Targ, and Harry Targ, *Plant Closings: International Context and Social Costs* (Hawthorne, NY: Aldine de Gruyter, 1988).

7. "The Hundred Largest U.S. Multinationals," *Forbes* (July 17, 1995): 274–76.

8. Robert Perrucci, *Japanese Auto Transplants in the Heartland: Corporatism and Community* (New York: Aldine de Gruyter, 1994).

9. Roger Bybee, "NAFTA's Hung Jury," *Extra!* (May–June 2004): 14–15.

10. Carolyn Perrucci and Robert Perrucci, "Unemployment," *Encyclopedia of the Life Course and Human Development* (Farmington Hills, MI: Gale, 2008).

11. Steve Lohr, "Debate over Exporting Jobs Raises Questions on Policies," *New York Times* (February 23, 2004).

12. Steve Lohr, "Offshore Jobs in Technology: Opportunity or a Threat?" *New York Times* (December 22, 2003).

13. Robert Perrucci and Earl Wysong, *The New Class Society: Goodbye American Dream?* (Lanham, MD: Rowman & Littlefield, 2008), 57.

14. U.S. Census Bureau News, U.S. Department of Commerce, http://www.census.gov/foreign-trade/PressRelease/.

15. Katherine S. Mangan, "A Shortage of Business Professors Leads to 6-Figure Salaries for New Ph.D.'s," *Chronicle of Higher Education* 47 (May 4, 2001): A12–13.

16. Robert Granfield and Thomas Koenig, "Pathways into Elite Law Firms: Professional Stratification and Social Networks," in *Research in Politics and Society*, vol. 4, *The Political Consequences of Social Networks*, eds. Gwen Moore and J. Alan Whitt (Greenwich, CT: JAI Press, 1992), 325–51.

17. Perrucci and Wysong, *The New Class Society: Goodbye American Dream?*, 14.

18. Perrucci and Wysong, *The New Class Society: Goodbye American Dream?*, 14.

19. William Greider, "Riding into the Sunset," *Nation* (June 9, 2005). See http://www.thenation.com/doc/20050627/greider.

20. Carolyn Perrucci, et al., *Plant Closings*.

21. "The Downsizing of America," *New York Times* (New York: Times Books, 1996), 80.

22. "The Downsizing of America," *New York Times*, 84.

23. "The Downsizing of America," *New York Times*, 59.

CHAPTER 3

1. Jennifer L. Hochschild, *Facing Up to the American Dream: Race, Class, and the Soul of the Nation* (Princeton, NJ: Princeton University Press, 1995), 72.

2. Robert Perrucci and Earl Wysong, *The New Class Society: Goodbye American Dream?* (Lanham, MD: Rowman & Littlefield, 2008), 65.

3. Lawrence Mishel, Jared Bernstein, and Sylvia Allegretto, *The State of Working America, 2004–2005* (Ithaca, NY: Cornell University Press, 2005), 137.

4. Ryan T. Helwig, "Worker Displacement in 1999–2000," *Monthly Labor Review* (June 2004): 54–68.

5. Seymour M. Lipset and Reinhard Bendix, *Social Mobility in Industrial Society* (Berkeley, CA: University of California Press, 1959).

6. Earl Wysong, Robert Perrucci, and David W. Wright, "A New Approach to Class Analysis: The Distributional Model, Social Closure, and Class Polarization." Presented at the 2002 meetings of the American Sociological Association, Chicago, IL; Earl Wysong and David W. Wright, "What's Happening to the American Dream: Sons, Daughters, and Intergenerational Mobility." Presented at the 2007 meetings of the Midwest Sociological Society, Chicago, IL; David Featherman and Robert M. Hauser, *Opportunity and Change* (New York: Academic Press, 1978).

7. Tiffani Chin and Meredith Phillips, "Social Reproduction and Child-Rearing Practices: Social Class, Children's Agency, and the Summer Activity Gap," *Sociology of Education* 77 (July 2004): 185–210.

8. Robert Perrucci and Earl Wysong, *The New Class Society* (Lanham, MD: Rowman & Littlefield, 1999), 182.

9. Annette Lareau, *Unequal Childhoods: Class, Race, and Family Life* (Berkeley, CA: University of California Press, 2003), 1–4.

10. U.S. Census Bureau, *Public Education Finances 2006* (Washington, D.C.: U.S. Government Printing Office, April 2008).

11. U.S. Department of Education, *Digest of Educational Statistics 2000* (Washington, D.C.: U.S. Government Printing Office, 2001).

12. "The Persisting Myth That Black and White Schools Are Equally Funded," *Journal of Blacks in Higher Education* 22 (Winter 1988–1999): 17–18, 20.

13. Jennifer L. Hochschild and Nathan Scovronick, *The American Dream and the Public Schools* (Oxford: Oxford University Press, 2003), 59–60.

14. Douglas Harris, "Lost Learning, Forgotten Promises," Center for American Progress, November 29, 2006 (www.americanprogress.org/issues/2006/11/lost learning.html).

15. Maureen Hallinan, "Tracking: From Theory to Practice," and Jennie Oakes, "More Than Misapplied Technology: A Normative and Political Response to Hallinan on Tracking," *Sociology of Education* 67 (1994): 79–91; Sally Kilgore, "The Organizational Context of Tracking in Schools," *American Sociological Review* 56 (1991): 189–203; Karl Alexander, Martha Cook, and Edward McDill, "Curriculum Tracking and Educational Stratification," *American Sociological Review* 43 (1982): 47–66.

16. David Fasenfest and Robert Perrucci, "Changes in Occupation and Income, 1979–1989: An Analysis of the Impact of Place and Race," *International Journal of Contemporary Sociology* 31 (1994): 203–33.

17. William Julius Wilson, *The Truly Disadvantaged* (Chicago: University of Chicago Press, 1987).

18. Carla O'Connor, "Race, Class, and Gender in America: Narratives of Opportunity among Low-Income African American Youths," *Sociology of Education* 72 (1999): 137–57.

19. Anita Chandra, Steve Martino, Rebecca Collins, Marc Elliot, Sandra Berry, David Kanouse, and Angela Miu, "Does Watching Sex on Television Predict Teen Pregnancy? Findings from a National Longitudinal Study of Youth," *Pediatrics* 122 (November 2008).

20. Jay P. Greene, "High School Graduation Rates in the United States," Institute for Policy Research, November 2001.

21. Randall Collins, *The Credential Society* (New York: Academic Press, 1979).

22. U.S. Department of Education, Digest of Educational Statistics, 2000; National Center for Educational Statistics (http://nces.ed.gov//programs/digest/d03/tables/dt249.asp).

23. Sara Rimer and Alan Finder, "Harvard to Aid Students High in the Middle Class," *New York Times* (December 11, 2007); Derek Thompson, "Financial Aid: How Top Schools Compare," http://images.businessweek.com/ss/08/02/0204_financial_aid/index_01.htm.

24. Alison Damast, "Tuition: Assistance for the Middle Class," *Business Week* (February 3, 2008); Mary Specht, "Financial Aid Can't Keep Pace," http://www.usatoday.com/news/education/2006-08-30-financial-aid_x.htm.

25. Karen W. Arenson, "Cuts in Tuition Assistance Put College beyond Reach of Poorest Students," *New York Times* (January 27, 1997); Richard Kahlenberg, ed., *America's Untapped Resource: Low Income Students in Higher Education* (New York: Century Foundation, 2003).

26. United for a Fair Economy, *Born on Third Base: The Sources of Wealth of the 1996 Forbes 400* (Boston, MA: United for a Fair Economy, February 1997).

CHAPTER 4

1. Gallup Poll. Available at http://www.pollingreport.com/institut.htm.

2. David Brooks, "Follow the Fundamentals," *New York Times* (November 27, 2007).

3. Lynnley Browning, "Study Tallies Corporations Not Paying Income Tax," *New York Times* (August 13, 2008).

4. Peter S. Goodman, "When Foreigners Buy Factories: Two Towns, Two Outcomes," *New York Times* (April 7, 2008).

5. Reported in John Miller and Ramon Castellblanch, "Does Manufacturing Matter?" *Dollars and Sense* (October 1988): 6–8.

6. Gabriel Thompson, "Meet the Wealth Gap," *Nation* (June 30, 2008): 18–27.

7. Mark Dudzic, "Time to Abandon Illusions about Democrats," *Labor Party Press* (January–February, 2005): 8.

8. David Croteau, "Challenging the 'Liberal Media' Claim," *Extra!* (July–August 1998): 9.

9. Mark Cooper, "Reclaiming the First Amendment: Legal, Factual, and Analytic Support for Limits on Media Ownership," in *The Future of Media,* ed. Robert W. McChesney, Russell Newman, and Ben Scott (New York: Seven Stories Press, 2005).

10. Francis X. Clines, "Fueled by Success, Buchanan Revels in Rapid-Fire Oratory," *New York Times* (February 15, 1996).

11. Clines, "Fueled by Success, Buchanan Revels in Rapid-Fire Oratory."

12. David Reinhard, "The Democratic Convention: In Search of Two Americas," *Oregonian* (July 29, 2004): B13.

13. Jean Hardisty, *Mobilizing Resentment: Conservative Resurgence from the John Birch Society to the Promise Keepers* (Boston, MA: Beacon Press, 1999).

14. "A Time for American Leadership on Key Global Issues," *New York Times* (February 11, 1998).

15. Leon Trachtman and Robert Perrucci, *Science Under Siege?* (Lanham, MD: Rowman & Littlefield, 2000).

16. Polling Report. Available at http://www.pollingreport.com/institut.htm.

17. www.beyonddelay.org.

18. Ron Nixon, "Earmarks Persist in Spending Bills for 2009," *New York Times* (June 22, 2008).

19. Daniel W. Drezner and Henry Farrell, "Web of Influence," *Foreign Policy* 145 (2004): 32–40; Ray Maratea, "The e-Rise and Fall of Social Problems: The Blogosphere as a Public Arena," *Social Problems* 55 (February 2008): 139–60.

20. Jessica Clark, "Power to the People: The Perils and Promise of Point-and-Click Politics," *In These Times* (December 2007): 20–23.

21. Eric Alterman, "Wall Street to Daily Papers: 'Drop Dead,'" *Nation* (February 11, 2008): 13.

22. "From the Left: More Than a Figure of Speech," *Extra! Update* (February 1996): 1.

23. Laura Washington, "Missing: Minorities in the Media," *In These Times* (March 2008): 17.

CHAPTER 5

1. Stephen Cornell and Douglas Hartmann, *Ethnicity and Race: Making Identities in a Changing World* (Thousand Oaks, CA: Pine Forge Press, 1998).

2. Robert Wuthnow, Sharing the Journey (New York: Free Press, 1994).

3. Robert Putnam, "Bowling Alone: America's Declining Social Capital," *Journal of Democracy* 6 (1995): 65–78.

4. Jane Hardisty, *Mobilizing Resentment: Conservative Resurgence from the John Birch Society to the Promise Keepers* (Boston, MA: Beacon Press, 1999).

5. Pippa Norris and Ronald Inglehart, "Supply, Demand, and Secularization," *Secular Humanism* (February–March 2007): 29–32.

6. Norris and Inglehart, "Supply, Demand, and Secularization," 31.

7. Milton Gordon, *Assimilation in American Life* (New York: Oxford University Press, 1964).

152   *Notes*

8. Daniel P. Moynihan, *The Negro Family: The Case for National Action* (Washington, D.C.: U.S. Government Printing Office, March 1965).

9. Lee Rainwater and William L. Yancey, *The Moynihan Report and the Politics of Controversy* (Cambridge, MA: MIT Press, 1967).

10. Adalberto Aguirre, Jr., and Jonathan H. Turner, *American Ethnicity: The Dynamics and Consequences of Discrimination* (New York: McGraw Hill, 1965), 23–24.

11. John Higham, *Strangers in the Land: Patterns of American Nativism, 1860–1925* (New Brunswick: Rutgers University Press, 1955).

12. U.S. Bureau of Census: www.census.gov/population/socdemo/education/cps2003/tab10-12.xls.

13. U.S. Bureau of Census, *2006 American Community Survey* (Washington D.C.: U.S. Government Printing Office, 2006).

14. Amy K. Glasmeier, *Poverty in America* (New York: Routledge, 2006).

15. Aguirre, and Turner, *American Ethnicity*, 65.

16. U.S. Bureau of Census, *2006 American Community Survey*.

17. U.S. Bureau of Census, *2006 American Community Survey*.

18. U.S. Bureau of Census, *2006 American Community Survey*.

19. Aguirre and Turner, *American Ethnicity*, 169.

20. U.S. Bureau of Census, *2006 American Community Survey*.

21. Roger Cohen, "Race and American Memory," *New York Times* (April 17, 2008).

22. Richard D. Kahlenberg, *The Remedy: Class, Race, and Affirmative Action* (New York: Basic Books, 1997); Richard D. Kahlenberg, "Class-Based Affirmative Action," *California Law Review* 84 (July 1996): 1037–99; Walter Benn Michaels, *The Trouble with Diversity: How We Learned to Love Identity and Ignore Inequality* (New York: Metropolitan, 2006).

23. Michael Omi and Dana Takagi, "Situating Asian Americans in the Political Discussion of Affirmative Action," in *Race and Representation: Affirmative Action*, eds. Robert Post and Michael Rogin (New York: Zone Books, 1998).

24. Jane Hardisty, *Mobilizing Resentment*, 161.

CHAPTER 6

1. Arlie R. Hochschild, "The Culture of Politics: Traditional, Postmodern, Cold-modern and Warm-modern Ideas of Care," *Social Politics* 2 (1995): 331–46.

2. U.S. Census Bureau, 2005, "2004 American Community Survey," Table 1101 (Washington, D.C.: U.S. Census Bureau); U.S. Census Bureau, 2006, "America's Families and Living Arrangements 2005," Tables 53, 57 (Washington, D.C.: U.S. Census Bureau).

3. U.S. Census Bureau, 2007, *Statistical Abstract of the United States: 2007*, Tables 584, 585 (Washington, D.C.: U.S. Census Bureau).

4. U.S. Census Bureau, 2007, *Statistical Abstract of the United States: 2007*, Table 574.

5. Center for the Advancement of Women, Progress and Perils: New Agenda for Women, 2003 (www.advancewomen.org).

6. Thomas M. Vander Ven, Francis T. Cullen, Mark A. Carrozza, and John Paul Wright, "Home Alone: The Impact of Maternal Employment on Delinquency," *Social Problems* 48 (2001): 236–57.

7. Elizabeth Harvey, "Short-Term and Long-Term Effects of Early Parental Employment on Children of the National Longitudinal Survey of Youth," *Developmental Psychology* 35 (1999): 445–59.

8. J. Stacey and T. J. Biblarz, "(How) Does the Sexual Orientation of Parents Matter?" *American Sociological Review* 66 (2001): 159–83.

9. U.S. Department of Labor, Current Population Survey, 2001, Employed Persons by Detailed Occupation, Sex, Race, and Hispanic Origin (2002b) (http://www.dol.gov).

10. B. R. Ragins and T.A. Scandura, "Antecedents and Work-Related Correlates of Reported Sexual Harassment: An Empirical Investigation of Competing Hypotheses," *Sex Roles* 32 (1995): 429–55.

11. Ann Crittenden, *The Price of Motherhood: Why the Most Important Job in the World Is Still the Least Valued* (New York: Metropolitan Books, 2001).

12. U.S. Department of Labor, Current Population Survey, 2001: Employed Persons by Detailed Occupation, Sex, Race, and Hispanic Origin (http://www.dol.gov).

13. A. S. Christensen, "Sex Discrimination and the Law," in *Women Working*, eds. A. H. Stromberg and S. Harkess (Mountain View, CA: Mayfield, 1988), 329–47.

14. Barbara F. Reskin and Irene Padevic, "Sex, Race, and Ethnic Inequality in the United States Workplace," in *Handbook of Sociology of Gender*, ed. Janet S. Chafetz (New York: Kluwer, 1999), 343–74.

15. Paula England, *Comparable Worth: Theories and Evidence* (New York: Aldine de Gruyter, 1992).

16. R. J. Steinberg and A. Cook, "Policies Affecting Women's Employment in Industrial Countries," in *Women Working*, eds. A. H. Stromberg and S. Harkess (Mountain View, CA: Mayfield, 1988), 307–28.

17. Institute for Social Research, University of Michigan, "U.S. Husbands Are Doing More Housework While Wives Are Doing Less," Press Release, March 12, 2002.

18. Arlie Hochschild, *The Second Shift* (New York: Viking, 1989).

19. Crittenden, *The Price of Motherhood*.

20. T. M. Beers, "Flexible Schedules and Shift Work: Replacing the '9-to-5' Work Day?" *Monthly Labor Review* 23 (2000): 33–40; Harriet Presser, "Nonstandard Work Schedules and Marital Instability," *Journal of Marriage and the Family* 62 (2000): 93–110.

21. Robert Perrucci and Shelley MacDermid, "Time and Control in a 24/7 Environment: Clock Time, Work Time, Family Time," in *Workplace Temporalities: Research in the Sociology of Work*, ed. Beth Rubin (Amsterdam: Elsevier, 2007), 343–68.

22. Lydia Saad, "No Time for R & R, Gallup Poll Tuesday Briefing," May 11, 2004 (www.gallup.com).

23. U.S. Bureau of Labor Statistics, Time Use Survey (Washington, D.C.: Bureau of Labor Statistics, 2004), Tables 1, 6.

24. Min Zhan and Shanta Pandey, "Economic Well-Being of Single Mothers: Work First or Postsecondary Education?" *Journal of Sociology and Social Welfare* 31 (September, 2004): 87–112.

25. Children's Defense Fund, *The State of America's Children, 2001* (Washington, D.C.: Children's Defense Fund, 2001).

26. *The State of America's Children, 2001.*

27. Children's Defense Fund, *The State of America's Children—Yearbook 1997* (Washington, D.C.: Children's Defense Fund, 1997).

28. "Statistical Abstract of the United States, 2006," 125th edition (Washington, D.C.: U.S. Bureau of the Census).

29. S. B. Kamerman, "Child and Family Policies: An International Overview," in *Children, Families, and Government: Preparing for the Twenty-first Century*, eds. E. F. Zigler, S. L. Kagan, and N. W. Hall (New York: Cambridge University Press, 1996), 31–48.

30. J. Overturf Johnson and B. Downs, "Maternity Leave and Employment Patterns: 1961–2000," *Current Population Report* (Washington, D.C.: U.S. Bureau of Census): 70–103.

31. James T. Bond, Ellen Galinsky, Stacy S. Kim, and Erin Brownfield, *National Study of Employers*. Families and Work Institute. Accessed 4/3/08 (http://families andwork.org/index.asp?PageAction=VIEWPROD&ProdID=137).

32. K. Smith, B. Downs, and M. O'Connell, "Maternity Leave and Employment Patterns: 1961–1995," U.S. Bureau of Census, Current Population Reports, 70–79. Accessed 4/3/08 (http://www.census.gov/prod/2001pubs/p70-79.pdf).

33. American Academy of Pediatrics, *Caring for Children: National Health and Safety Performance Standards as Guidelines for Out-of-Home Child Care Programs* (Elk Grove Village, IL: American Public Health Association and American Academy of Pediatrics, 1992).

34. Bond, et al., *National Study of Employers.*

35. Claire Renzetti and Daniel Curran, *Women, Men and Society*, 4th edition (Boston: Allyn and Bacon, 1999).

36. Robert Perrucci and Carolyn C. Perrucci, "Unemployment and Mental Health: Research and Policy Implications," in *Research in Community and Mental Health: Mental Disorder in Social Context*, ed. James R. Greenley (Greenwich, CT: JAI Press, 1990), 237–64.

CHAPTER 7

1. Amy K. Glasmeier, *An Atlas of Poverty in America: One Nation, Pulling Apart, 1960–2003* (New York: Routledge, 2006).

2. *Geography Matters: Child Well-Being in the States* (Washington D.C.: Every Child Matters Education Fund, April 2008).

3. National Commission on Children, *Beyond Rhetoric: A New American Agenda for Children and Families* (Washington, D.C.: U.S. Government Printing Office, 1991).

4. U.S. Bureau of Labor Statistics, Women in the Labor Force: A Datebook. Report 996 (Washington, D.C.: September 2006). Retrieved March 31, 2008 (http://www.bls.gov/cps/wlf-databook2006.htm).

5. B. Miller, "Household Futures," *American Demographics* 17 (March 1995): 4, 6.

6. U.S. Department of Health and Human Services, Administration on Children, Youth, and Families, Child Maltreatment 2005 (Washington, D.C.: U.S. Government Printing Office, 2007). Retrieved March 31, 2008 (http://www.acf.hhs.gov/programs/cb/pubs/cm05/index.htm).

7. Olivia Golden, Pamela J. Loprest, and Shiela R. Zedlewski, *Parents and Children Facing a World of Risk: Next Steps toward a Working Families' Agenda*. Roundtable Report. The Urban Institute, March 10, 2006 (http://www.urban.org/url.cfm?ID=311288).

8. Katherine S. Newman and Victor T. Chen, "The Crisis of the Near Poor," *Chronicle of Higher Education* 54 (October 5, 2007): B10.

9. Howard Karger, "America's Growing Fringe Economy," *Dollars and Sense* (November/December 2006): 16–21.

10. Robert Perrucci and Earl Wysong, *The New Class Society: Goodbye American Dream?* (Lanham, MD: Rowman & Littlefield, 2008), 184.

11. Alison Leigh Cowan, "Counting the Homeless to Help End Their Plight," *New York Times* (February 26, 2008): 6.

12. "Striving to Keep Up Appearances," *Baltimore Sun* (March 2, 2006): 11A.

13. Lizzy Ratner, "Homeless in New Orleans," *Nation* (February 25, 2008): 13–18.

14. U.S. Census Bureau, Current Population Survey 2005, U.S. Department of Health and Human Services, 2005 (http://aspe.hhs.gov/health/reports/05/uninsured-cps/).

15. Mary Ann Schwartz and BarBara Marliene Scott, *Marriages and Families: Diversity and Change* (Upper Saddle River, NJ: Pearson Education, Inc., 2003).

16. A. D. Mancini, D. L. Pressman, and G. A. Bonanno, "Clinical Interventions with the Bereaved: What Clinicians and Counselors Can Learn from the Changing Lives of Older Couples Study," in *Spousal Bereavement in Late Life*, eds. D. Carr, R. M. Nesse, and C. B. Wortman (New York: Springer, 2006), 255–78.

17. Rich Hogan and Carolyn C. Perrucci, "Producing and Reproducing Class and Status Differences: Racial and Gender Gaps in U.S. Employment and Retirement Income," *Social Problems* 45 (1998): 528–49; Rich Hogan and Carolyn C. Perrucci, "Black Women: Truly Disadvantaged in the Transition from Employment to Retirement Income," *Social Science Research* 36 (2007): 1184–99.

18. Richard K. Caputo, "Grandparents and Coresident Grandchildren in a Youth Cohort," *Journal of Family Issues* 22 (2001): 541–56.

19. Administration on Aging, "A Profile of Older Americans: 2001," (http://www.aoa.gov/prof/Statistics/profile/2001/2001profile.pdf).

20. Gail Hunt, Carol Levine, and Linda Naiditch, *Young Caregivers in the U.S.: Report of Findings*, September 2005 (Bethesda, MD: National Alliance for Caregiving).

21. "Elderly Abandoned at Hospitals: Granny Dumping Is a Variation of Baby-on-Doorstep," *Chicago Tribune* (November 29, 1991): sec. 1, 27.

22. U.S. Department of Justice, Prison Statistics. Bureau of Justice Statistics (www.ojp.usdoj.gov/bjs/).

23. U.S. Department of Justice, Prison Statistics.

24. U.S. Department of Justice, Prison Statistics.

25. Henry Fernandez, "Phoning Home: High Cost Calls Hinder Prisoner Rehabilitation," Center for American Progress. April 7, 2007 (http://www.americanprogress.org/issues/2007/04/phoning_home.html).

26. B. Owen, "Perspectives on Women in Prison," in *Women, Crime and Criminal Justice*, eds. C. M. Renzetti and L. Goodstein (Los Angeles: Roxbury, 2001), 243–54.

27. Devah Pager, "Creating Second Chances," *Pathways: A Magazine on Poverty, Inequality, and Social Policy* (California: Stanford University, Summer 2008): 29–32.

28. Barry Krisberg and Susan Marchionna, "Attitudes of U.S. Voters toward Prisoner Rehabilitation and Reentry Policies," *Focus*, National Council on Crime and Delinquency, April 2006.

CHAPTER 8

1. Amy Glasmeier, *An Atlas of Poverty in America: One Nation, Pulling Apart, 1960–2003* (New York: Routledge, 2006); Alison Leigh Cowan, "Counting the Homeless to Help End Their Plight," *New York Times* (February 26, 2008): 6.

2. Paul Krugman, "Jobs/Wages Today," *New York Times* (December 28, 2007).

3. "Is Trade the Problem?" *New York Times* (April 27, 2008).

4. David Sirota, "The Upside of Nationalism," *In These Times* (April 28, 2008): 32–33, 47.

5. American Society of Civil Engineers, Report Card on America's Infrastructure (http://www.asce.org/reportcard/2005/index.cfm).

6. Robert Perrucci and Earl Wysong, *The New Class Society: Goodbye American Dream?* (Lanham, MD: Rowman & Littlefield, 2008).

7. Noreen Connell, "Underfunded Schools: Why Money Matters," *Dollars and Sense* (April 1998): 14–17, 39.

8. Noreen Connell, "Underfunded Schools."

9. Ralph Nader, "Testimony on Corporate Welfare." U.S. House of Representatives Committee on the Budget, June 30, 1999. On the Internet at www.nader.org/releases/63099.html.

Index

About the Authors

Robert Perrucci is professor of sociology at Purdue University. He has served as president of the Society for the Study of Social Problems, associate editor of the *American Sociological Review*, and editor of the *American Sociologist*, *Social Problems*, and *Contemporary Sociology*. In 2005 he received the Lee Founders Career Achievement Award from the Society for the Study of Social Problems.

Carolyn C. Perrucci is professor of sociology at Purdue University. She has coauthored or coedited three books: *Marriage and the Family: A Critical Analysis and Proposals for Change*, *Women in Scientific and Engineering Professions*, and *Plant Closings: International Context and Social Costs*. She has contributed to numerous journals, including *American Sociological Review*, *International Journal of the Humanities*, *Journal of Marriage and the Family*, *Social Problems*, *Sociology and Social Research*, *Sociology of Education*, and *The Sociological Quarterly*.